TEIGNMOUTH
AT WAR
1939 to 1945

Written & Published by Viv Wilson

First Published October 2000
© Viv Wilson 2000

Designed by Images, Teignmouth
Printed by Exeprint, Exeter
ISBN: 0 9539523 0 4

ACKNOWLEDGEMENTS

Arts Round Teignbridge - £300 grant towards publication costs
Bill Barter - drawing two plans of the river as remembered by Harry Sealey
John Ware - providing material
Teignmouth Museum - access to their archives and loans
Tim Mole - help and advice about Home Guard and military matters
Pauline Rossi - patient monitoring of text
Arthur Smith - practical guidance
David Markham - permission to reproduce painting of the Fairey Fulmar
Peter Ridler - successful mediator between the computer and me
Rotary Club of Teignmouth - information and support
Jim Stowers - eleventh hour checking
Dominic Jeffery - a knight in shining armour
Everyone who shared memories and photographs

It is a great privilege to publish this collection. Sincere thanks to all those who contributed photographs, records and memories in such generous style

BIBLIOGRAPHY

Exeter - Newton Abbot: A Railway History by Peter Kay
History of Teignmouth by Grace Griffiths
Shaldon 1939 - 45 by Tim Mole
Teignmouth's Haldon Aerodrome by Keith A Saunders
Teignmouth by H J Trump
War Poems and After by G Lewis Cook
Teignmouth Grammar School - the First 50 Years

DISCLAIMER
All information other than the Official Records included in the book has been recorded in good faith by Viv Wilson who offers it as collected memories from those who were around at the time.

Written & Published by Viv Wilson

DEDICATION

This book is dedicated to all those whose courage,
selflessness and dedication to duty helped to preserve freedom
and liberty for post-war generations of Teignmouth
and of Great Britain

Six decades ago our forebears stood on the brink of the Second World War. Almost everyone over 60 years of age has some enduring memory of it, the rest of us rely on impressions found in books and films, photographs and handed-down stories.

This volume is the only serious attempt to illuminate the suffering of Teignmouth and its people during six years of war. Loss of life and destruction touched each family at a time when everyone in the community knew one another.

Post war generations can use the book to make discoveries: the replacement house that looks newer than its neighbour: a block of flats erected for those who lost their cosy terraced town houses. Detailed knowledge allows numerous connections.

Wholesale destruction exposed old and out of repair property. Much of it was demolished in the 1960s and many local people hold the opinion that the eradication of the old centre was a serious error of judgement.

Proposals for Teignmouth's refurbishment were too ambitious to become reality. In the town centre new Municipal Buildings with a 1000 seat Conference Hall were envisaged and a circular pavilion at Esplanade with an 850 seat concert hall. An open-air swimming pool 132 feet long was to be built near the Lighthouse and the slopes on both sides of Broadmeadow Valley would be covered with houses. The plans did not materialize.

For the second time in its history, Teignmouth rose from the ashes, unaware that the 1960s would mark the final fling of prosperity through tourism in the 20th century.

The story of Teignmouth at War needed to be told. It may help the town's young people understand the sacrifice and endurance of former generations. A potent mix of memories and pictures bring truth and reality home to roost. The passing of time does not diminish the power of images to shock - and to touch the heart.

Viv Wilson July 2000

Foreword by Cllr Fred Tooley

Mayor of Teignmouth in the year 2000

TW Lee Edwards, Clerk to Teignmouth Urban District Council recorded that between July 1940 and February 1944, the district experienced 21 Raids and 460 Alerts. Over one thousand incendiaries and 79 high explosive bombs were dropped.

The death toll was 79 people and there were 151 casualties. The newly completed Hospital was destroyed. Of the 2957 houses in the town, 228 were completely demolished and 2250 were damaged. Only 479 houses were unscathed.

"In proportion to its size, Teignmouth stands high on the list of towns which have suffered from enemy action. It is indeed heavily battle scarred, but planning for its restoration has been entrusted to Professor SD Adshead...and its townspeople look forward to the time when once again it will take its place among the leading health resorts of Britain"

Although Viv Wilson is not a Teignmothian, she became involved with the resort in the mid 1950s. Since moving here to live in 1986, Viv has expended a great deal of energy in generating a deep awareness and appreciation of Teignmouth through its townspeople and visitors. Her books and slide shows are of great interest – familiar faces and events of long ago rekindling fond memories amongst local people.

This record of wartime Teignmouth is to be recommended to you.

1939

Preparations for War

In 1938 Brigadier Morrison, Teignmouth's Honorary Air Raid Precaution Organizer, ordered a supply of sledge hammers, picks, wheelbarrows, handsaws, hurricane lamps, ladders and numerous other pieces of equipment. Its non-arrival was an early indication of what was to come. Teignmouth began – and endured most of its war totally ill-equipped on all fronts.

ARP Literature sent out with Rate Demands encouraged 319 volunteers at the first appeal. Throughout the winter months they travelled to Newton Abbot for a total of 60 hours training in how to cope with anticipated poison gas attacks. Third class rail fare and 10/6 (53p) daily subsistence was allowed.

Teignmouth Urban District Council ordered trenches to be dug in open ground and sandbags to be requisitioned. A massive supply of bleach was ordered. The efficiency of an electric siren was tested during variable weather conditions and by day and night. A civilian Respirator was installed at the Hospital. A Millbay Laundry delivery van became a make-shift ambulance.

The Ministry of Health ordered a survey of surplus accommodation and it was found the town had sufficient space to cope with an estimated 8597 people. Arrangements for dealing with death by war, transportation of bodies, mortuary and burial arrangements were discussed in council.

TUDC estimated the cost of preparing buildings for use as First Aid posts, refuge rooms, Decontamination centres and public shelters. When Devon County Council failed to respond to the estimates, TUDC wrote to the County Clerk to express their dissatisfaction.

"TUDC views with apprehension the entire lack of progress in the Air Raid Precaution Scheme for Teignmouth since the passing of the Act of Parliament in 1937".

Turn that light out!

Teignmouth prepared itself for the Blackout as war was declared. All street lamps were switched off and effective coverings fitted to every window lest the slightest beam became a target. Tape was glued across windowpanes to restrict flying glass. Morrison shelters replaced kitchen tables and Anderson shelters were entrenched in many gardens.

As trainloads of Teignmothians left home to serve in the Armed Forces, hundreds of children evacuated from London poured in by rail. After the first raid in July 1940, locals began to leave Teignmouth for safer places.

Food and fuel went on ration. Gas masks were issued to each person including babies. Everyone had to carry an identity card. Posters advised the public to be alert to the possibility of spies "Walls have Ears.." and "Careless talk costs Lives.."

In June 1940 the War Office printed 14,300,000 copies of an advisory leaflet to the people of Great Britain. "If the Invader comes – what to do and how to do it" incorporated seven golden rules. It is reproduced on pages 26 & 27. Read it and ask yourself how would you have reacted to it.

Local girl Joan Hill (R) joins the knitting circle in the sunshine on the Den

The first air raid would soon shake Teignmouth to its foundations

Territorial Army at Hazeldown

For two weeks in August 1939 the 3rd and 5th Survey Regiments of Bristol's Territorial Army Royal Artillery set up camp at Hazeldown. With war ominously near uniforms had been issued. The regiment was boosted by a huge influx of volunteers who needed last minute preparation for their wartime role as the "eyes and ears" of our artillery and to locate enemy guns.

Training on Haldon included the use of trigonometry and a grid system to fix survey points enabling the artillery on a wide front to fire accurately at the same target.

In the field, Observers operated from well forward positions. Enemy guns could be located at any time by taking microphone recordings. At night, spotters picked up flashes from enemy guns. All the information was rapidly co-ordinated by the surveyor's computing teams and fed back to Artillery Command.

T A Camp in Hazeldown Field August 1939

The 3rd & 5th Survey Regiments of Bristol Territorial Army Royal Artillery
camped for two weeks

When John Caines retired to Teignmouth he decided to relocate the wartime site. Back in 1939 his Regiment arrived in Teignmouth by rail, marched up a long hill from the Station and into a muddy lane leading to a field of tents. The Ness and skyline in John's original photographs were valuable clues in confirming that the site had been at Hazeldown. A post war football field, it is now part of the school.

The Regiment took part in a Sunday church parade that was a regular feature of life in the town at that time. After the service they marched from church to the Den. The resort was crowded with people enjoying the last few days of peace. Ten months later many of the Regiment were amongst the 330,000 troops evacuated from Dunkirk.

Site of the TA camp-now Hazeldown School Field

Teignmouth Grammar School

In 1938 a squadron of the Air Defence Corps was founded with 65 cadets. Two years later it was renamed Air Training Corps 60 Squadron and acceptance was no longer limited to pupils. ATC cadets gained experience of flying planes at Haldon Aerodrome.

In 1939 the Grammar School had to make space to integrate staff and pupils of Haberdasher Aske's School for girls from London. The attics and changing rooms, cloakrooms and even the space between the kitchen and refrigeration room were pressed into service as classrooms. Four different lessons ran simultaneously in the Assembly Hall. Ingenious time-tabling ensured that both sets of pupils continued with a full work programme.

Haberdasher pupils made use of the craft block, sports field and gymnasium in the mornings whilst formal class lessons were given to local children. In the afternoon, the classes changed over.

The school had its own brick built bomb shelter. Mr Leslie Bossom was the only member of staff called up for active service.

Mr Sidney Silverston the Headmaster deplored the tendency for pupils to leave school early to fill positions vacated by those entering the Armed Forces.

Air Training Corps 60 Squadron

HD Gourd beside his bus, Teignmouth Railway Station Yard 1930s

Three Gourd brothers (L-R) Philip, George and Dougie.

Gourd's of Bishopsteignton

Gourd's transport and haulage business operated all through the war years. One of the few firms to be issued with new buses, their vehicles were often used for military purposes and several evacuations.

Dougie Gourd and Harry Harris were removing a lorry load of furniture collected from a bombed-out house when an enemy plane headed low towards them on the seafront. Dougie hastily changed direction and began to reverse at speed. The lorry was strafed with machine gun fire and some of the bullets entered the driver's cab but both escaped injury.

In 1939 a touring exhibition of replica Crown Jewels sponsored by the Daily Mirror was brought to the Triangle. Young Philip watched with interest from the bus stop as several large but light crates were unloaded into the premises, currently a newsagents. The imitations made from papier-mache and coloured glass were impressive.

Shortly after the declaration of war, two city gents arrived at the house in a black limousine and asked HD Gourd to transport the crates to Cornwall. This was puzzling for the crates were now so heavy that it took two men to lift them. A Police motorcyclist kept Gourd's van under surveillance on its journey. Once the crates were safely stored below ground in Bodmin Gaol, the city gents breathed an enormous sigh of relief. Could a switch between the replicas and the real thing have taken place?

This intriguing possibility remained a secret within the family for many years.

Teignmouth Pier

Local pleasure boats 1930s

Fred Sealey's *Princess Mary* (centre) Jack Hitchcock's *White Heather* (R) and Ern Nathan's *Sea Belle* (L) Pixie Matthews' *Britannia* is beyond

Fun lovers at the Pier would revel in concerts, beauty shows and talent contests, waltz and quick-step the night away, change into beach wear, fish for mackerel, catch pleasure steamers, play penny machines, have their fortunes told, buy candy floss, lunch or afternoon tea …or simply wallow in the balmy breezes. Two paddle steamers, the Duke and Duchess of Devonshire used this point for passengers.

Pier end Landing Stage

Meg Niblett

Meg was a waitress at the Pier Restaurant in 1939. Soon after 11am on the morning of Sunday September 3rd Mr Angliss the Manager told Meg that Britain was at war. She must go out to the landing stage to tell anglers and pleasure boat passengers the news and inform them that if they remained on the Pier it was at their own risk.

Pier staff were expected to fulfil their normal duties to the end of the day.

Coastguards

Chief Tom Bloomfield (L) and Bert Parrick at Ivy Lane. These two men kept watch from the Coastguard look-out at the foot of Cliff Walk day and night through the war years and witnessed many incursions. On one occasion a German pilot made a slow approach, as if on photographic reconnaissance. He flew upriver and returned past the Ness before dropping bombs in the sea. Eye witnesses say that it appeared that the pilot had no wish to damage Teignmouth.

Some local people camped out overnight up in Eastcliff meadows rather than risk being buried alive at home.

The Sprey Point look-out could not be reached from the sea wall, blocked by anti-invasion barricades. The railway line was used for access and there was great sadness on two separate occasions when Auxiliary Coastguards Tom Barnes and Frank Riddle were killed by trains.

Whalebone Arch

In 1987 the local Press enquired into the fate of the whalebone arch erected by Pike Ward in 1924.

AG Avent, a man with considerable local knowledge had the answer.

In 1940 when he was a platoon sergeant in the Home Guard, the Army placed a machine gun in the bank that was higher and thicker then. The whalebone arch interfered with the line of fire and was removed to Broadmeadow. It was re-erected on land between the gas works and railway by one of the allotment holders, creating interest for a time in the 1950s.

Old Maid's Walk or Perch at Eastcliff 1930s

Teignmouth Coastguards kept watch day and night from the look-out hut on the left behind the other whalebone arch. When the bones were found to be rotting after the war they were removed to Broadmeadow Tip.

Halfway Café at Sprey Point

Between the wars Norman Boyce and his wife Jessie ran the popular rendezvous. Visitors played bagatelle and ping-pong al fresco or lazed under sun shades.

The couple also worked as gardener and housekeeper for Lady Nelson Harness, formerly a theatrical Gibson Girl residing at Derncleugh House on Holcombe Head.

Jessie aged 90 recalled the day when orders to remove all their equipment immediately from the café were received from the War Office. They hurried down but found that the Durham Light Infantry had already cleared Sprey Point for anti-invasion measures. All of their equipment had been thrown into the sea.
The café did not re-open.

1940

Facsimile copy of original records

AIR RAIDS ON TEIGNMOUTH
LIST OF CASUALTIES.

NAME	SEX	APPROXIMATE AGE	ADDRESS	KILLED OR INJURED	RAID
MEDLAND, Joyce	F	16 yrs.	48, Parson St., Teignmouth.	K S.I. (died from injuries)	7th July, 1940. In sea off Teignmouth Pier.
MATTHEWS, James,	C	14	2, The Strand, "	S.I.	"
BARTES, Peggie	C	9	3, Stanley St. "	S.I.	"
GARRARD, Jina	C	14	61, Second Avenue, "	S.I.	"
VICKERY, Tony	C	12	47, Teign Street, "	S.I.	"
CANN, Betty	C	14	3, New Quay St. "	L.I.	"
BUTLER, Margaret	F	30	44, Fore St. Shaldon.	L.I.	"
TIBBS, Emily	F	59	22, Bickfords Lane, Teignmouth.	L.I.	"
MORTIMORE, Teresa	C	13	21a, Parson St. "	L.I.	"
WILLIAMS, Mrs.	F	77	5, Daimonds Lane, "	L.I.	"
HANCOCK, Sylvia	C	13	64, Second Avenue, "	L.I.	"
MARTIN, Mrs.	F	51	45, Crossley Moor, Kingsteignton.	L.I.	"
RODWELL, P.J.	M	15	13, Coombe Vale, Teignmouth.	L.I.	"

Joyce Medland

Joyce, a cheerful girl of 16 was the first victim of enemy action in Teignmouth. On 7th July 1940 she was hit by a piece of shrapnel out by the Pier and died in Teignmouth Hospital the following day. Local people were deeply shocked and Joyce's name became etched in many minds ever afterwards.

Raid 1

Sunday 7th July 1940 at 6.55pm   **Teignmouth Seafront**

2 High Explosives
1 death and 12 casualties.
Shattered window glass but otherwise no serious damage to property

Many people were strolling about enjoying the evening air on the Pier and shore when an enemy plane (possibly a Junkers-Ju 88) approached from the west, dived to a height between 500 and 1000 feet and dropped two bombs in the sea close to the Pier. The raid was so sudden that the siren was not sounded. Flying bomb segments injured twelve people, seven of whom were children.

The casualties were taken to an Emergency Ward established on the ground floor of Teignmouth Hospital.

Machine gun bullet embedded in a roll of 6d bathing cabin tickets

Jim Matthews

Jim aged 14 was one of a group of boys on the Pier during the first raid. The bomb exploded into lethal splinters and Jim was hit in the leg. His friend Reg Barnes and the candy floss lady were amongst the casualties. Six months passed before Jim could resume normal life.

After sixty years as a boatman, Jim was still driving the river ferry at weekends in the new millennium. The deep scar from the knee wound is a significant reminder of a harrowing time.

South Devon Mobile Column 1940

Trained volunteers under the leadership of Donald Sharpe formed the Teignmouth Platoon of the South Devon Mobile Column in 1940. The Columns were intended as back-up after the loss of more than 60,000 troops and a huge number of weapons at Dunkirk in 1940. Training took place on Haldon and Dartmoor with Regular Forces from Newton Abbot.

Each man was issued with a rifle and had priority issue of weapons including a Vickers machine gun, Tommy gun and a plentiful supply of hand grenades. The Column also had use of a Devon General bus that reported for duty each Sunday morning.

In the event of invasion, the Column was to become the first line of defence behind the beaches. Their orders were to retreat to a hide-out on Haldon from where they could act as a Guerrilla force.

Back L-R Dyer. I Purchase. B Steer. RH Doel. S Wadsworth.
J Blatchford. Burgoyne. Johns.
Centre L-R K Blackler. J Gaskin. DH Sharpe. R Lang. J Roberts
Front L-R W Harvey. P Camp. J Bonetto. D Sherbourne

Bill Harvey

Bill and his friends Derek Sherbourne and John Bonetto were interviewed at the Dawlish Inn to become Local Defence Volunteers. After claiming they were 18, the three 16 year olds were taken into the South Devon Mobile Unit. Bill also joined ATC 60 Squadron. There were times when he rushed home to change uniform from ATC to Home Guard with only moments to spare.

The harsh reality of war came home to roost one evening in July 1940. Bill was on the river beach where people were lying about enjoying the sunshine. A plane was seen circling overhead. Someone thought at first that it was dropping leaflets but it turned out to be bombs. It came as a shock. Teignmouth's first raid had started!

The Army was ordered to give the Mobile Unit volunteers some experience of what might happen if England was invaded. During an exercise in the area of New Rd, a soldier passed by on his motorbike. Bill shied a bag of flour masquerading as a hand grenade and the soldier fell off the bike. Later whilst Bill was hiding out in a hedge at Hazeldown, a revolver was suddenly held to his head and the soldier growled "You're dead!" His stealthy approach taught Bill to watch his back at all times!

When LDV became better organized, Bill went as a gunner on the Ness where a pair of 4.7 RN guns were situated. He also worked one of the searchlights beside the road leading up to Ness House. Searchlight duty was considered high risk because the beams could be used as a firing line for enemy aircraft.

Ron Doel

I was just a young chap enjoying myself with friends at the start of the the war. I sat on my seat in the field and gave much thought to the men in their pleasure boats shouting "trips round the bay" only last year and wondered what those brave chaps would be thinking as they navigated their fragile boats towards France to evacuate thousands of troops.

I remember 7th July 1940 as if it were only yesterday. My friend Rene and I were sitting on top of the Jubilee Shelter at Eastcliff enjoying the fine Sunday evening and watching a plane overhead. I was showing off my skills as a plane spotter, declaring the aircraft to be one of ours. I was safe in this assumption because there had been no air raid warnings.

Suddenly there were two loud explosions from bombs dropped either side of the Pier entrance. From our bird's eye view of the seafront we could see there was a panic. People ran for cover as a large cloud of smoke rose into the clear blue sky. We made for Mordref Hotel where some ladies were crying with shock. Several were injured in the first of many raids on our small town. The siren had gone off just after the bombs dropped. Half an hour later when the all-clear sounded, we walked along to the Pier and realised that if a bomb had hit the entrance, the disaster would have been far greater.

The townspeople were deeply disturbed and could talk of nothing else. From the moment my father's shop door was opened the next morning, a brisk trade in suitcases began. All those who came to Teignmouth thinking it would be safe, were leaving the sinking ship.

I watched soldiers setting up machine guns and Bren guns. We needed anti-aircraft guns but the Country just did not have any to spare for such a small town. I decided to join the Local Defence Volunteers, later known as the Home Guard. Rifle ammunition and hand grenades were stored in our HQ at the rear of Dawlish Inn. We made a very swift exit when a bomb dropped a few yards away one night!

Our home, Elmonte House in Buckeridge suffered a broken window and smashed roof tiles from a shower of machine gun bullets during the raid on 10th January 1943. One bullet missed my head by a couple of inches as I lay on the floor. When the all-clear sounded, I looked out of the window and saw several columns of smoke rising into the clear afternoon sky. Parts of the town seemed to be shrouded in haze. Dad asked me to go and see if the shop was damaged. I felt very apprehensive on the way down but the town centre and shop had escaped damage.

I walked to the seafront and was horrified to see a crowd and the fire brigade by Powderham Terrace where two of the houses were no longer standing. One was the home of my great friend Peter Rendell. I asked one of the firemen if there were any survivors and was told that a lady (Peter's mother) was alive but injured.

I was extremely upset - my sister Dorothy came down the hill to meet me and confirm the sad news about the loss of Peter. If I had not slept late that morning, I would have been with him at his home.

On my next day off, I looked at the damage suffered by our poor town. The area to the north was in ruins. Gone were the cottage homes of the many inhabitants. Within two weeks I was working in a Signals Workshop at Exeter airfield. I often think about that fateful Sunday when I survived two close shaves in one day and feel eternally grateful.

Issued by the Ministry of Information *in co-operation with the War Office and the Ministry of Home Security.*

If the

INVADER

comes

WHAT TO DO — AND HOW TO DO IT

THE Germans threaten to invade Great Britain. If they do so they will be driven out by our Navy, our Army and our Air Force. Yet the ordinary men and women of the civilian population will also have their part to play. Hitler's invasions of Poland, Holland and Belgium were greatly helped by the fact that the civilian population was taken by surprise. They did not know what to do when the moment came. *You must not be taken by surprise.* This leaflet tells you what general line you should take. More detailed instructions will be given you when the danger comes nearer. Meanwhile, read these instructions carefully and be prepared to carry them out.

I

When Holland and Belgium were invaded, the civilian population fled from their homes. They crowded on the roads, in cars, in carts, on bicycles and on foot, and so helped the enemy by preventing their own armies from advancing against the invaders. You must not allow that to happen here. Your first rule, therefore, is :—

(1) IF THE GERMANS COME, BY PARACHUTE, AEROPLANE OR SHIP, YOU MUST REMAIN WHERE YOU ARE. THE ORDER IS "STAY PUT".

If the Commander in Chief decides that the place where you live must be evacuated, he will tell you when and how to leave. Until you receive such orders you must remain where you are. If you run away, you will be exposed to far greater danger because you will be machine-gunned from the air as were civilians in Holland and Belgium, and you will also block the roads by which our own armies will advance to turn the Germans out.

II

There is another method which the Germans adopt in their invasion. They make use of the civilian population in order to create confusion and panic. They spread false rumours and issue false instructions. In order to prevent this, you should obey the second rule, which is as follows :—

(2) DO NOT BELIEVE RUMOURS AND DO NOT SPREAD THEM. WHEN YOU RECEIVE AN ORDER, MAKE QUITE SURE THAT IT IS A TRUE ORDER AND NOT A FAKED ORDER. MOST OF YOU KNOW YOUR POLICEMEN AND YOUR A.R.P. WARDENS BY SIGHT, YOU CAN TRUST THEM. IF YOU KEEP YOUR HEADS, YOU CAN ALSO TELL WHETHER A MILITARY OFFICER IS REALLY BRITISH OR ONLY PRETENDING TO BE SO. IF IN DOUBT ASK THE POLICE-MAN OR THE A.R.P. WARDEN. USE YOUR COMMON SENSE.

III

The Army, the Air Force and the Local Defence Volunteers cannot be everywhere at once. The ordinary man and woman must be on the watch. If you see anything suspicious, do not rush round telling your neighbours all about it. Go at once to the nearest policeman, police-station, or military officer and tell them exactly what you saw. Train yourself to notice the exact time and place where you saw anything suspicious, and try to give exact information. Try to check your facts. The sort of report which a military or police officer wants from you is something like this :—

"At 5.30 p.m. to-night I saw twenty cyclists come into Little Squashborough from the direction of Great Mudtown. They carried some sort of automatic rifle or gun. I did not see anything like artillery. They were in grey uniforms."

Be calm, quick and exact. The third rule, therefore, is as follows :—

(3) KEEP WATCH. IF YOU SEE ANYTHING SUSPICIOUS, NOTE IT CAREFULLY AND GO AT ONCE TO THE NEAREST POLICE OFFICER OR STATION, OR TO THE NEAREST MILITARY OFFICER. DO NOT RUSH ABOUT SPREADING VAGUE RUMOURS. GO QUICKLY TO THE NEAREST AUTHORITY AND GIVE HIM THE FACTS.

IV

Remember that if parachutists come down near your home, they will not be feeling at all brave. They will not know where they are, they will have no food, they will not know where their companions are. They will want you to give them food, means of transport and maps. They will want you to tell them where they have landed, where their comrades are, and where our own soldiers are. The fourth rule, therefore, is as follows :—

(4) DO NOT GIVE ANY GERMAN ANYTHING. DO NOT TELL HIM ANYTHING. HIDE YOUR FOOD AND YOUR BICYCLES. HIDE YOUR MAPS. SEE THAT THE ENEMY GETS NO PETROL. IF YOU HAVE A CAR OR MOTOR BICYCLE, PUT IT OUT OF ACTION WHEN NOT IN USE. IT IS NOT ENOUGH TO REMOVE THE IGNITION KEY; YOU MUST MAKE IT USELESS TO ANYONE EXCEPT YOURSELF.

IF YOU ARE A GARAGE PROPRIETOR, YOU MUST WORK OUT A PLAN TO PROTECT YOUR STOCK OF PETROL AND YOUR CUSTOMERS' CARS. REMEMBER THAT TRANSPORT AND PETROL WILL BE THE INVADER'S MAIN DIFFICULTIES. MAKE SURE THAT NO INVADER WILL BE ABLE TO GET HOLD OF YOUR CARS, PETROL, MAPS OR BICYCLES.

V

You may be asked by Army and Air Force officers to help in many ways. For instance, the time may come when you will receive orders to block roads or streets in order to prevent the enemy from advancing. Never block a road unless you are told which one you must block. Then you can help by felling trees, wiring them together or blocking the roads with cars. Here, therefore, is the fifth rule :—

(5) BE READY TO HELP THE MILITARY IN ANY WAY. BUT DO NOT BLOCK ROADS UNTIL ORDERED TO DO SO BY THE MILITARY OR L.D.V. AUTHORITIES.

VI

If you are in charge of a factory, store or other works, organise its defence at once. If you are a worker, make sure that you understand the system of defence that has been organised and know what part you have to play in it. Remember always that parachutists and fifth column men are powerless against any organised resistance. They can only succeed if they can create disorganisation. Make certain that no suspicious strangers enter your premises.

You must know in advance who is to take command, who is to be second in command, and how orders are to be transmitted. This chain of command must be built up and you will probably find that ex-officers or N.C.O.'s, who have been in emergencies before, are the best people to undertake such command. The sixth rule is therefore as follows :—

(6) IN FACTORIES AND SHOPS, ALL MANAGERS AND WORKMEN SHOULD ORGANISE SOME SYSTEM NOW BY WHICH A SUDDEN ATTACK CAN BE RESISTED.

VII

The six rules which you have now read give you a general idea of what to do in the event of invasion. More detailed instructions may, when the time comes, be given you by the Military and Police Authorities and by the Local Defence Volunteers; they will NOT be given over the wireless as that might convey information to the enemy. These instructions must be obeyed at once.

Remember always that the best defence of Great Britain is the courage of her men and women. Here is your seventh rule :—

(7) THINK BEFORE YOU ACT. BUT THINK ALWAYS OF YOUR COUNTRY BEFORE YOU THINK OF YOURSELF.

(52194) Wt. /   14,300,000 6/40 Bw.

Anti-Invasion Barricades

Barbed wire and scaffolding barriers installed along the sea wall in 1940

Anti-Invasion barriers at Esplanade

An amateur snap of a guillemot also records the barricades

Novel climbing frame

Youngsters cheerfully ignored signs prohibiting use of the beach

Twins Gladys and Fred Laurie

Amateur film was unobtainable for most of the war. Local photographer Ivy Hindley was also a pianist and often accompanied Gladys, an expert fancy whistler in neighbourhood entertainment

Doreen Kavanagh

I remember a very frightening visit to Teignmouth when I was 8. Mum, Dad, my little sister in her pram and my older brother and I left home in Highweek for a day trip on the train to the seaside. Two people who were staying in our home came along - Iris, an evacuee from Gravesend and Ron down from Bradford to learn about new machines at Vickary's Woollen Mills in Bradley Lane where my father was Supervisor.

A huge blockade of scaffolding had been built between the beach and prom but we managed to find space for our picnic. Afterwards we paddled in the sea. Later when Dad and his friend went off to check train times and probably have a pint, my brother asked to go on the Pier. Mum refused - money was tight in our household and she did not approve of gambling.

Instead we walked along the front to watch a large boat heading into the harbour. As we approached the ferry shelter, an aircraft appeared overhead and we saw black things coming from it. Ron and Iris realised that it was an enemy plane dropping bombs and dived for cover in the ferry shelter, banging their heads together in their hurry to get under the seat. I just stood there not knowing what to do. Mum was trying desperately to get my little sister free from her pram straps. The noise, smell, screaming and broken glass petrified us. When it was all over, we rushed back along the seafront to be met by a frantic Dad.

How glad we were not to have been allowed to go on the Pier where someone had been fatally injured. On our way back to the station we saw the chaos caused by shrapnel, glass and rubble. We were very thankful to be going home all together and did not visit Teignmouth again until long after the war ended. My little sister refused to wear car seat belts until it became compulsory. The horror of that day remains as vivid as ever.

Railway

The outbreak of war had an immediate effect on the railway and Teignmouth Station witnessed a big exodus of holidaymakers. Passenger numbers dropped significantly whilst the emergency reduced timetable was in operation. Teignmouth recorded 60,423 passengers in 1940 its worst year, when anti-invasion measures included barbed wire along the sea wall beside the line.

The lack of visitors was counterbalanced by an influx of evacuees who used the Holiday Line. By 1942, Summer Saturday Extras were re-introduced and by the final year of war, services had virtually returned to normal.

The railway was targeted because of its significance as a main route for Plymouth-bound freight. The signal box at the Station was raked with machine gun fire but there were no injuries.

Many houses close to the line suffered direct hits yet there was only one occasion when enemy action caused temporary closure. On July 5th 1941, a delayed action bomb exploded close to the rails near Salcombe Dip on Newton Rd. In the same area on November 3rd 1942 the line was dislocated but quickly restored.

It is remarkable that the stretch of railway line through Teignmouth escaped with so little damage.

GWR Holiday Line

A King Class steams along the stretch close to where an enemy plane strafed a loco with machine gun bullets a few years earlier

Cyril Coleridge

On 14th May 1940, a quiet and peaceful day, my family was being photographed at the west door of St James Church on the occasion of my brother's wedding. I was almost thirteen and unaware of the desperate trouble the British Expeditionary Force was experiencing in France. The threat of invasion was imminent. Council employees were busy building defences on the beaches and sea front and roadblocks at entrances to town. At school we filled sand bags - more fun than studying!

The newly formed Local Defence Volunteers had little in the way of arms. The Commander called a meeting for parents of 3rd Teignmouth Scouts, St James Troop to seek permission to ask for volunteers to train as messengers reporting to the local police if parachutes landed. I was willing. Every fifth or sixth night we were out on Haldon. The seriousness of the situation did not strike me at the time - it was an adventure!

After the overnight duties ended, we continued to act as messengers for the Home Guard and spent many hours on weekend exercise consisting mostly of standing around waiting and getting very cold.

3rd Teignmouth Scouts St James Troop on the Vicarage lawn

Back row L-R Pillar : ? ? Howard : Crook : ? ? ? ? Locke : Plummer
Middle L-R Britton : Barnes : Coleridge : Winch : Newtstead : Rev Crabb : Stowers Scown : Waldron : Mardon : Scown
Front L-R Collins : Gaylor : Trust : ? : Banham : Ray : Clode : Babbage : ? : Bennington

1943 L-R Henry Jones, Dougie Winter and Cyril Coleridge

At work on a 35 foot sea plane tender in Morgan Giles Shipyard

Tip and run air raids began. Bombs fell on Speranza Grove, Bitton Park Rd and Gloucester Rd one Sunday afternoon just as I arrived at St James vestry. The church was filled with a cloud of dust.

I dashed for home at Chelsea Place, not knowing what I might find. The bomb that fell on Gloucester Rd where I had passed a few minutes earlier had exploded beside the auxiliary water tank. Mr Parker (known as Buller) was in a doorway attending to Mr Pile in a severe state of shock. He asked me to run to the Kangaroo Inn in Teign St for a bottle of brandy and say that he would pay for it next day. It was a Sunday and I was only a lad - the licencee showed some reluctance but complied. I ran back but found the casualties had been taken to hospital. My mother returned the brandy the next day.

As I dug potatoes at my father's allotment at Broadmeadow, an aircraft flew very low over the hedge with guns firing. I saw the pilot very clearly - I did not wave! It turned down river at the gas works and headed out to sea.

As an apprentice at Morgan Giles Shipyard I was helping to build pinnaces for the Royal Navy on the top floor of the big shed known as the toy shop. A sheet of corrugated iron had worked loose in the corner of the roof. One Saturday afternoon as a strong wind swept down river it suddenly became detached and rattled across the roof sounding like machine gun fire. In seconds everyone had disappeared except one man who was aware of the situation. He just stood and laughed his head off - it was hilarious at the time!

Morgan Giles Shipyard

Wartime expansion of Morgan Giles Shipyard was rapid. Bulley's Boat Builders moved across from the quay to join the workforce that rose at peak times to 180 including 20 women. The yard was fully occupied with Admiralty and RAF demands requiring, at times, a 7 day working week. The workforce demonstrated their tenacity throughout.

The yard handled refits for numerous Admiralty craft and RAF Air Sea Rescue launches. It also maintained the Kingswear Flotilla of Motor Torpedo Boats manned by Free French crews including the 1st Lieutenant son of Charles de Gaulle. A register of complex, specialized craft essential to this country's coastal defences built and maintained in the yard during those critical years includes:

6 small trawlers
4 naval cutters
6 motor pinnaces 35 foot in length
4 harbour defence motor launches 72 foot in length and capable of 12 knots
50 assault landing craft and fast motor pinnaces
5 pinnaces of 60 foot length fitted with a large derrick designed as torpedo recovery craft for the Royal Naval Air Service
8 Motor Torpedo Boats of 70 foot length capable of 40 knots with a pair of torpedo tubes mounted forward and a power operated gun mounted aft
12 harbour launches 36 foot in length constructed and lowered through hatches from the upper floor of the big shed for launching
2 MFVs sixty one and a half foot length that eventually went to the Scottish fisheries

The first Vosper-type MTB to be laid down by Morgan Giles in 1941

The 72 foot ship, the first of 8 to be built at the yard had a port torpedo tube and scalloped-cut portion of fore deck and side to allow clear passage for the torpedo. This ship (240) was allocated to Royal Netherlands Navy.

Dunkirk

On 3rd June 1940 the shipyard took in two requisitioned motor tugs, the *Valiant* and the *Heron*. The latter brought clay barges down the river Teign. Three more Teignmouth motor boats- *Britannia*, *Shamrock* and *Golden Wings* together with *Meteor* and *Eclipse* from Torquay were also brought in. All were made ready to sail for Dover to assist in the evacuation of British Expeditionary Forces from Dunkirk.

None of them made it. Four vessels set off from Teignmouth. *Heron* blew an exhaust flange off Portland and was towed into Weymouth by *Meteor*. Both were ordered home. *Valiant* put in at the Isle of Wight to refuel and also received orders to return. *Eclipse* reported to guard ship off Weymouth and after being detained for two hours was sent home to Torquay. The eight men who put to sea were paid £2 each.

Motor tug *Heron* at work on the Teign in the 1930s

She made Dorset but not Dunkirk

Minor Raids 2, 3 & 4

Monday 8th July 1940 at 2.19pm　　　　**Seafront**

5 High Explosives
No deaths or casualties
No damage to property

The day following Teignmouth's first raid a single unidentified plane flew in from the south at 1500 feet and dropped five bombs in the sea near the Pier.

21st October 1940 at 10.45 pm　　　　**Lindridge area of Bishopsteignton**

The records do not include details of planes or bombs. There were no casualties

12th December 1940 at 10.40pm　　　　**Wood area of Bishopsteignton**

No record of any casualties

The Harbour

Within months of the outbreak of war, Teignmouth found herself in the front line as she had been in Napoleonic times. Coastal trade was poor yet coal ships with barrage balloons for protection against air attacks continued to call. Neither key targets- Morgan Giles Shipyard and the railway line sustained significant damage but there were several near misses causing damage to property nearby.

In 1940 the Lifeboat Station ceased after more than 80 years service and was to stay closed for half a century. The Ministry of War ordered closure of the public right of way along the harbour beach. The Admiralty requisitioned small boats and on payment of £200 took over the harbour. Teignmouth Harbour Commission was ordered to take immediate action to repel invasion from seaplanes. Despite few resources and manpower the Royal Navy established a River Patrol of retired local sailors and fishermen.

Posts for the boom can still be seen on either side of the estuary

The estuary was protected by a boom of wire, two and a half inches thick. Large spherical iron pellets interspersed with smaller ones studded its length. Each night the River Patrol used the *Hindustan* (originally *Britannia* pleasure boat) to "close" the river mouth between the Point and Shaldon House.

Before putting to sea, local fishermen reported to Captain Rees the resident Naval Officer based at the Royal Hotel. They would be informed of a Recognition Signal using two letters of Morse Code allowing re-entry to the harbour after dark. The signals changed daily. Approaching fishing boats were challenged by a signal from a hand torch on the shore. The crew replied with the Recognition Signal and passed over the boom at full throttle.

1st Platoon Teignmouth Home Guards

Training invariably took place two nights each week and on Sundays. An Assault Course was set up in field near Labrador where the men could practice the use of hand grenades. Their camp was down a steep lane at Maidencombe. The Devon General bus that was at their disposal could not easily cope with the gradient so the HGs would have to push it as it reversed uphill.

As the Army went further afield, so the Home Guard took over local defence. The rifle range was at Starcross - possibly the location of the photograph above. Sometimes an Army lorry from Denbury Camp transferred them to the range and at other times, they went in the Devon General bus. The five tunnels between Teignmouth and Dawlish were guarded at both ends when invasion fears were at their highest in 1940.

Dawe's potent cider brewed in Bishopsteignton was not unknown to the Platoon. One morning in particular, the amber liquid flowed faster than usual and that afternoon, not a single target was hit!

1941

Facsimile copy of original records

NAME	SEX	APPROXIMATE AGE	ADDRESS	KILLED OR INJURED	RAID
HOOK, Leslie George	M	29	Seaman, Royal Navy. Teignmouth. 47, Second Avenue,	K	2nd March, 1941. 5 H.E.Bombs, Mill Lane, & Avenues.
HOOK, Dorcas Irene	F	29	" " "	K	"
HOOK, Delphin Mary	C	3	" " "	K	"
FIELD, Frank	M	54	47, Second Avenue, Teignmouth.	K	2nd March, 1941. (contd)
FIELD, Elsie Jane	F	53	" " "	K	"
CORPS, Gordon	C	11	"Lynfield", Kingsdown, "	L.I.	"
SMITH, Mary	F	69	" " "	L.I.	"
BARNES, Ethel	F	49	45, Second Avenue, "	L.I.	"
BARNES, Elizabeth	F	75	" " "	L.I.	"
PHARE, Evelyn	F	34	49, " "	L.I.	"
PHARE, Sheila	C	14	" " "	L.I.	"
HERBERT, Jane Elizabeth	F	66	"Heswall", Kingsdown, "	K	8th May, 1941. (10 H.E.Bombs, Hospital and Kingsdown,Mill Lane)
WITHEROW, Rosa	F	56	5, Dagmar St. Shaldon.	K	"
MILNER, Beatrice	F	49	"Bareys", Dawlish Rd. Teignmouth.	K	"
MUNDY, Bessie	F	55	"Coombe Bank", Landscore Rd. "	K	"
COTMORE, Mary Louise	F	60	2, Foresters Terrace, "	K	"
TATCHELL, John Francis	M	80	"Claremont", Bishopsteignton.	K	"
MOORE, Eliza	F	75	"Fairlight", Paradise Rd.Teignmouth.	K	"
BEWORTHY, Rosina	F	69	31, Brunswick St. "	K	"

Facsimile copy of original records

NAME	SEX	APPROXIMATE AGE	ADDRESS	KILLED OR INJURED	RAID
JAMES, Beatrice (Nurse)	F	17	Alberta Mansions, Teignmouth.	K	8th May, 1941 (contd)
TAYLOR, Muriel (Nurse)	F	22	52, Gentwood Rd, Hayton, Nr.Liverpool.	K	do.
BRUNS, Olgar (Nurse)	F	26	"Formosa", Torpark Rd, Torquay.	K	do.
BEARHAM, Percy	C	10	20, Hutchings Way, Teignmouth.	L.I.	do.
STEVENS, Carliss	C	6	23, Daimonds Lane, do.	L.I.	do.
SULLIVAN, M. (Private)	M	19	C.Coy, 70th Batt. Queens Royal Rifles.	L.I.	do.
HERBERT, Henry Edward	M	50	"Heswall", Kingsdown Estate, Teignmouth.	I.	do.

* The following are from Hospital Records as being treated in Hospital, but were not officially reported to A.R.P.

NAME	SEX	APPROXIMATE AGE	ADDRESS	KILLED OR INJURED	RAID
* TURTAN, Rev. B.	M			Shock, cuts & bruises.	do.
* PRIVE, Mrs.	F			do.	do.
* HATHAWAY, Mrs. A.	F			Shock	do.
* PICKE, Mrs.	F			do.	do.
BELLAMY, P.	M	84	"Cathays", Yannon Drive, Teignmouth.	L.I.	2 H.E. Bombs, Exeter Road, 24th October, 1941.
BELLAMY, Kathleen	F	32	do.	L.I.	do.
BELLAMY, Albert	M	34	do.	L.I.	do.
ROFF, George William	M	82	do.	L.I.	do.
EVEL, THOMAS EDRE D	M	45	Mount Everest, Exeter Road, "	K	do.
SHACKELL, GEORGE	M	19	6102621, 70th Queen's Regt. Haldon Military Camp.	K	do.
BOTLEY, Pte. L.J.	M		6103863, do. and 38, Warren Road, Addiscombe, Croydon.	L.I.	do.

Haldon Aerodrome

The Air Ministry requisitioned the 1920s Aerodrome at the outset of war. When invasion fears were high, beach huts transferred from the seafront became a blockade to repel troop-carrying enemy gliders. Runways were extended to include most of the adjacent golf course. Haldon Tea House became a billet for Guards whilst WRNS were accommodated in local guest houses.

In 1941 the Admiralty commissioned the Aerodrome as HMS Heron II, a satellite of RNAS Yeovilton. After several minor mishaps the runways were lengthened in 1942. Further improvements included the installation of Tarmac hardstanding and Sommerfield steel tracking. The RNAS carried out target practice in Lyme Bay. Wind-sock targets called drogues were towed by Blackburn Skuas. One ditched in shallow water between the Pier and Jubilee Shelter after either engine failure or friendly fire in error - there was always uncertainty. Several years passed before the fuselage was removed.

Admiralty Operations were frequently affected by poor weather conditions at Haldon and in May 1943 the unit moved to Charlton Hawthorne. The Aerodrome was placed under a care and maintenance programme. An RAF Gliding School Number 84 was formed and for the last two years of war, local Air Cadets received elementary training at Haldon Aerodrome.

AIR VIEW OF AERODROME, GOLF COURSE & RIVER, TEIGNMOUTH

W.R. PARKHOUSE
"The man who put TEIGNMOUTH on the air-map."

William R Parkhouse MBE

The foresight of the Aerodrome's founder who ran Agra Engineering in Devon Arms Yard, has considerable significance when viewed in the context of war. Early in the 1930s William Parkhouse encouraged Whitney Straight to develop the Straight Corporation that was responsible for Britain gaining a nucleus of trained pilots and newly built airfields. Without his vision this country would have entered the affray at a considerable disadvantage.

It is appropriate that this volume should acknowledge the strong connections he had with Teignmouth and honour the memory of William R Parkhouse MBE.

A Gipsy Moth piloted by William R Parkhouse at Haldon Aerodrome

Haldon Tea House became a billet for Aerodrome Guards

Raid 5

15th February 1941 at 7.55pm   **Ringmore area of Shaldon**

No record of any casualties

Raid 6

Sunday 2nd March 1941 at 8.03pm   **Mill Lane & The Avenues**

5 High Explosives
5 deaths and 7 casualties
Three houses on Second Avenue destroyed and significant damage to property

Second Avenue where numbers 45, 47 & 49 were demolished by the raid

A direct hit on number 47 killed a family of five: a Royal Navy seaman home on Leave, his wife and 3 year-old daughter and the wife's parents

The first raid to incur loss of property began at three minutes past eight on a Sunday evening. Five bombs fell in the Mill Lane area causing considerable damage. A gas main burst into flames and the electric light main was also affected. Within thirty minutes, the Rescue Party, three First Aid Parties and the Road Repair Squad had reported for duty.

About 100 men from the Company of Buffs and Queens stationed in Teignmouth assisted the Rescue Party under the directions of the Leader, Mr John S Scown. Air Raid Wardens did excellent work in soothing people in the densely populated area.

The Fire Service, unable to stop the fire in the gas main, heaped earth on it to control the flames until it was blanked off two hours later. Enemy aircraft flew off low over the River Teign escaping a burst of Hotchkiss Tracer delivered by RN River Patrol.

Putting on brave faces in Second Avenue

Teignmouth & Shaldon War Weapons Week in March 1941

March Past watched from the steps of the Royal Hotel by the Chairman of Teignmouth Urban District Council, Cllr H Irish and visiting Military

Ada Hook nee Williams

Ada was an 18 year old apprentice draper at Frasers in 1939. The Wellington St shop, now Hitchens, fitted three thick timbers inside a storeroom in the yard. This was supposed to suffice as an air raid shelter.

All women were mobilized to a Factory or the Forces at 19 unless they were unfit. Ada's father Edwin, one of Teignmouth's Rescue Party would not agree to her going in the Forces so she went to Heathcoat Amory's Tiverton factory. Another local girl, Doris Robbins also went and they were taught to make parachutes. The girls had to cut out and patch any flaws found in the balloon silk. Visiting airmen told them of a parachutist who looked upwards as he floated down and saw a blue patch. He had a nasty moment thinking that he was seeing the sky through a hole!

Ada was moved to Smith's technical instruments factory where three long camouflage-covered buildings stood next to Cheltenham's famous race course. New arrivals were assessed in their first week. Ada was offered a job in the office but rejected it, preferring to work alongside her new-found friends making altimeters for aircraft. It was precision work involving the use of micrometers measuring down to one thousandth of an inch.

When her small, capable fingers were noticed, Ada was moved up as a jeweller embedding industrial diamonds into altimeter levers. The only difficulty the task presented was keeping the eyeglass in place. A piece of hurriedly improvised headgear did the trick!

The diamonds were separated by type for use in exit or entrance beds. They were very small and had to be handled with brass tweezers. One slipped under beading at the counter's edge. When Ada endeavoured to recover it, the beading worked loose releasing dozens of "lost" diamonds. These had to be sorted by X-Ray before they could be re-used.

Ada hoped to be allowed to come home when VE Day arrived but she was delayed at the factory until after VJ Day in August 1945.

Ada (R) and friends at Smith's Instruments Factory, Cheltenham

Teignmouth Electric Lighting Company Platoon

ELC's platoon - officially E Company 9th Devon Home Guard - pictured on the quay by local photographer Hindley's of the Triangle

Back Row	**L-R**	Foster : Durman : Sanders : Furler : Howe
Middle row	**L-R**	Bryant : Brealey : Shapter : Cornelius : Northcott : Drew
		Satchell : Bush : Kelsall : Retallick : Clarke : Rendle
Front row	**L-R**	Palmer : Matthews : Grant : Guscott : Andrews

Ian Frost with Salvation Army hat and bugle

The Salvation Army Band was kept up by women stalwarts through the war

Ian Frost

I was about 6 or 7 and Lottie Trout was spoiling me as usual. We were on our way to buy some cherryade at the post office and provision shop at the far end of Coombe Road. Suddenly I heard a loud rat-tat-tat sound I'd never heard before. She pushed me into the gutter and dear, large Lottie threw herself on top of me - the first and only time I'd ever been machine-gunned!

The plane, we heard later had followed the line of Coombe Rd. Lottie was a stalwart member of the Salvation Army - clearly her prayers were heard so we picked ourselves up and she bought me that cherryade!

My grandmother looked rather like a petite Queen Mary and was every bit as indomitable. During the early days of the war Mrs Frost proclaimed that she had always taken her walk around the Den and Hitler certainly wasn't going to stop her. On one occasion when she was on the Prom, the air raid warning blared out. This did nothing to deter her progress. The only concession she made to the situation was to put up her small parasol - which was bright red!

Raid 7

Thursday 8th May 1941 at 2.15am   **Teignmouth Hospital,**
Mill Lane & Kingsdown

10 High Explosives
11 deaths and 4 casualties
Hospital in ruins and damage to about 40 houses nearby

Ten bombs of varying calibre dropped on Teignmouth Hospital and neighbouring Kingsdown Estate. Two fell in the hospital grounds and three on the women's ward, children's ward and the nurses' quarters. Three nurses and seven patients died. Four other patients were injured.

Rescuers searched for survivors with moonlight and hand torches as their only sources of light. Beds were buried beneath huge pieces of masonry, girders, tiles and debris from the ruined hospital. The front façade was one of the few walls to remain intact after the raid.

Five bombs fell on Kingsdown Estate where Heswall had a direct hit killing a woman of 60. Her body had been thrown into the garden by the force of the explosion.

Teignmouth Hospital raid 8th May 1941

ARP Warden and policeman inspect the pitiful remnants of metal bed frames

An Alert sounded at 11.30pm. Nucleus parties of all services were standing by in their respective depots but three hours passed before the raid began. The Council Road Repair Squad assisted Rescuers recover fatalities. Rescue Parties from Newton Abbot, Shaldon and Dawlish evacuated patients from Teignmouth to Newton Abbot Hospital.

Rescue Party Leader John Scown's ability to quickly appreciate all the implications of an involved situation was praised. The quick, methodical and efficient work of St John Ambulance Brigade and First Aid Parties was also mentioned in Brigadier Morrison's ARP report that also pays tribute to the Nursing Staff.

"They were splendid. All had experienced a heavy shock and strain. Despite this, the Matron, Sister and Nurses provided information in regard to the location of buried casualties with precision that enabled the Leader of the Rescue Party to do his work with the minimum of delay. The value of this coolness under shock and strain cannot easily be exaggerated."

Hospital buildings

Teignmouth Hospital

The £17,000 hospital had two 10-bed wards, four private wards, an operating theatre and X-ray facilities. Its completion represented years of strenuous fund-raising by townspeople. Lady Cable of Shute House performed the official opening ceremony in 1925. Alternative accommodation was found at Hermosa House following the raid that destroyed all but one section of the original building. The Physiotherapy and Radiology departments currently use this section, incorporated into the replacement hospital opened in 1954.

North Wall of Teignmouth Hospital

The plaque records that it was destroyed in 1941 and rebuilt in 1953-54

Heswall, adjacent to the hospital was destroyed by a direct hit

Minor Raids 8, 9 & 10

Thursday 15th May 1941 at 5.49am **Sea near the Pier**

Unknown number of High Explosives No casualties or damage recorded

Wednesday 11th June 1941 at 7.13pm **Railway Line and Hole Head tunnel**

Unknown number of High Explosives No casualties or damage recorded

Saturday 5th July 1941 at 2.40am **Salcombe Dip on Newton Rd**

6 High Explosives No casualties but some damage

Four of the six bombs landed in gardens and fields north of Newton Rd causing slight damage to three houses and destroying a cornfield at Ash Hill Farm. Another exploded near the railway bank and the sixth, a delayed action bomb exploded spontaneously six hours later cutting rail tracks and telegraph lines and causing a crater three feet wide by fifteen deep.

1941
A temporary hospital was established in Hermosa House

From back L-R
Nurses Hannaford : Ridd : Letheran
Oats : ? : Causley
Widge : Cowling : Pearson

Temporary Hospital Hermosa House

Nurses and workmen steal a few moments from their endeavours to be photographed during the conversion of Hermosa House. Workmen include Cecil Hatherly, W Webber, Jack Coombes, Harold Webber and Donald Allen

Donald Sharpe

When Teignmouth Hospital suffered an air raid in the early hours of the morning, the South Devon Mobile Column of Home Guard heard the bombs and immediately went to offer their assistance. A scene of total devastation was complicated by the presence of a crowd of onlookers. The ARP warden refused the offer of help and a bemused Lt Sharpe and his 8 men returned to base.

When invasion seemed imminent the platoon moved from their HQ at Dawlish Inn to Murley Grange at Bishopsteignton. The unit was transported in a Devon General passenger bus that, in the event of invasion was to be covered in camouflage paint and netting. Every Sunday at 9am, they set off to rendezvous with the Army for training on Haldon or Dartmoor.

Don as Battalion Gas Officer went to Salisbury Plain for instruction in dealing with the effects of mustard, tear and phosgene gas. He returned with phials of mustard gas and tubes of a type of barrier cream. The platoon was shown how to cover areas of exposed skin with the cream. *continues overleaf*

Unfortunately for Don, mustard gas penetrated a small area on his wrist and within the hour, a red tomato-like blister appeared. The Medical Corps based at Camp Reception station in Woodway Rd had no experience of gas blisters. They decided to lance it. Some of the fluid escaped and caused a fresh cluster of blisters to rise along his arm.

Every day for six weeks, Don had to suspend his duties as deputy Finance Officer for Teignmouth Urban District Council and report to the Medics. The treatment was basic: when his arm did not heal, it was held in front of a gas fire in a bid to dry the weeping blisters. A variety of ineffective lotions were applied. Eventually a tube of an everyday ointment purchased over the counter of the local chemist shop did the trick!

Few families escaped adversity. For Don and his wife Lorna it was the loss of a baby son and daughter brought on prematurely by air raids on two separate occasions. The girl, born in the maternity unit of a local Nursing Home died within the day and the boy lived less than a week. Happily, they were blessed with two more daughters.

The Sharpes' wartime home was with Lorna's parents, the Smallcombes at Cornubia. One night as Don stood on its south-facing terrace he saw an enemy plane flying down river and the sudden flash of the bomb door as it opened to release its deadly load. Two bombs fell at Shaldon - one in the river and the other close to St Peter's Church.

Each area of the town had its own ARP warden with the authority to immobilize cars in the interests of security. Don's War Office approved vehicle had to be ready for instant call-out and was not subject to civil laws. One night, the ARP warden phoned to advise him that he had removed the distributor arm to immobilize the car. The warden's actions were rewarded with a strong ticking off!

The river Teign was a useful landmark for enemy aircraft based at Cherbourg, 90 miles across the Channel. Sometimes as many as 8 swept in low over the sea, the sound of anti-aircraft guns dotted along the coastline heralding their approach. Daylight raids on Teignmouth ended when 5 of 8 were shot down on one such sortie.

Humour was an invaluable companion during the darkest of days. Two stories, both bordering on the apocryphal, were relayed at the time and remain locked in local memory. A lady enthroned in her timber lean-to toilet had a close encounter with a cannon shell. These deadly devices, about the size of a pocket torch could pass through brick walls. The shell shot in one side and out the other, passing literally before her eyes. The lady was shaken but unscathed.

The other story concerns a member of the Home Guard on security duty at Shaldon Bridge. A man approached. "Halt! Who goes there? Let's see your ID." The card was displayed but he couldn't read it properly. "Here! Hold my rifle whilst I get my glasses out!"

Raid 11

Friday 24th October 1941 at 9.15pm   **Yannon Drive - Exeter Rd**

2 High Explosives
2 deaths and 5 casualties
Widespread damage of varying degrees to property

One of the bombs calculated at about 50 kilos fell on Exeter Rd between Yannon Drive and Mount Everest Lodge killing a civilian and a serviceman.

A second fell 50 yards away on the Grammar School playing field. Both made small craters and caused minor damage. Windows were shattered and doors blown out across a mile from the point of impact. A voluntary group called Sitting Case Cars conveyed casualties between Hospital or First Aid posts and their homes or to accommodation with friends.

Mount Everest Lodge the morning after the raid on 24th October 1941

The River Beach festooned with barbed wire against invaders

Unperturbed by fears of invasion - Alfie Dodd, Janet Robbins and Eric Searle

GREETINGS

from

TEIGNMOUTH

and

SHALDON

✷ ✷

The Brunswick Printing Co prepared Christmas cards to be sent to members of the armed forces.

It included individual messages from churches of St Peter's at Shaldon, the Baptists, Gospel Hall, Congregationalists, St James', St Michael's, Salvation Army, Methodists, Our Lady and St Patrick as well as Cllr H Irish, Chairman of TUDC

Peribank on the junction of Yannon Drive and Exeter Rd

A householder sorts the belongings of her family home

After the raid in October 1941, Bgdr Morrison made a further plea for equipment for the Rescue Party who struggled to search a large number of damaged properties for victims with only three Stadium lamps at their disposal. Their entitlement was for seven.

"This difficulty was accentuated as the hand lamps damaged by the raids of March and May have not been replaced despite frequent reminders"

G Lewis Cook who lived in Shaldon for many years was a successful artist and poet. In 1984 he published a book called War Poems and After. The following poem was included in its pages

Air Raid

At first a low insistent wail
Impinges on the senses.
It rises and falls-rises and falls
Rises to a screech and falls to a moan
Screeching, moaning, screeching, screeching, scream,
The screams above all else prevail.
It dies
And drags a horrid silence in its trail.

Dread sound that stuns and mortifies
Now spurs to fevered action.
Now drives the knocking limbs and jangling nerves
To urgency and frantic stumbling haste,
Drives from out the mind all thoughts save one,
The thought that's mirrored in each pair of eyes,
To live
And cheat the loosened furies in the skies.

Ensues an awkward pregnant pause,
Leaden footed interim
That counterfeits a calm and loosens tongues
While ears and eyes still strain at nothingness,
Straining, striving to catch the sights and sounds
That every living soul abhors.
But hark!
There now the barrage in the distance roars.

Like rolling thunder still remote
As earth and air give battle.
The rumbling, rumbling, grumbling tumult grows
'Til sudden thund'rous booming close at hand
Bursts reverberating over head.
Piercing the roaring of canon's throat
Is heard
A desperate plane's high pitched and whining note.

Full fury of earth and sky
Are indeed unleashed at last.
Louder, louder drums that thund'rous boom,
Insistent, awful, ceaseless drumming boom
Enjoined with strident shrieks and sudden blasts
That rend the aching air and terrify
And stun
As pendant minutes barely stagger by.

Quite suddenly the sound has ceased:
The quivering air is empty.
Now minutes pass in apprehensive hush
Except where watchers fight the frequent fires.
As from uneasy slumber raised faint hope
Awakes and stirs within each throbbing breast
Until
At last by shrilling "Raiders Past" from threat released.

2.4.44

Alice Cross BEM

Alice was 44 when she joined the British Red Cross Society serving it throughout the war years. She also undertook firewatching duties.

In 1942, a bomb fell in the garden of her Bitton St home damaging it so badly it had to be pulled down. "From this disaster came the desire to give thanks for a life spared" said Alice. In the same year, Alice and Kathleen Warne were the first women to be admitted to the choir of St Michael's Church.

In 1945, Alice was founder member and Honorary Secretary of the "Service for Others" Committee that spent £50 on a party for 210 elderly residents of the town to mark the first Christmas of Peace. Alice devoted the remainder of her long life to helping the town's elderly people. She died a few months after reaching her century in 1995.

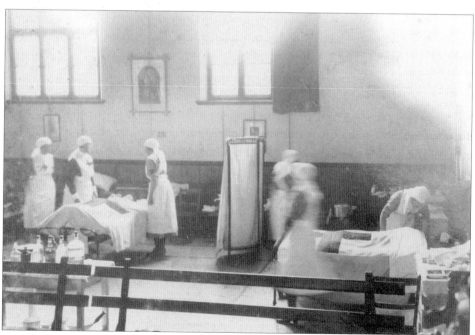

1930s Teignmouth Branch of British Red Cross training for emergency

WRNS & CO at Kittoes, Bishopsteignton

Rita Menghini nee Boyne

Rita (centre) and other local girls named Day, Hodge, Hexter, Radford, Beddow, Clode and Drew joined the Women's Royal Navy Service. Rita became an Officers' steward in the property adjoining the Marina Hotel at the south end of Powderham Terrace. The Royal Navy used the Marina as a Mess. During one particular raid, lots of people rushed into the requisitioned hotel to take cover.

An Army Sergeant taught them to parade on the Point car park. Much of their time was spent on cleaning duties. WRNS from further away were involved with armoury work at Haldon Aerodrome where young pilots attached to the Fleet Air Arm from RNAS Yeovilton were trained. Groups of about 12 pilots stayed for 10 days at a time.

Each day, a large RN transport lorry driven by a local coach driver called Jones conveyed the servicemen and women up to the Aerodrome where WRNS dispensed tea and stacks of sandwiches prepared in the Mess. One day, the lorry was the target of machine gun fire as it was passing the cemetery but all escaped injury. Rita never felt in fear for her life.

The WRNS had their share of fun and every Saturday night danced with Ratings at the London Hotel. After Powderham Terrace was bombed, the unit moved out to Kittoes in Bishopsteignton.

On July 4th 1942, Rita did her best to ignore the gaping hole in the bedroom ceiling, donned her bridal gown, stepped over a heap of rubble from a bomb in Mulberry St and set off for her wedding to Ernest Menghini serving in the Royal Navy. It was six years before Ernest completed his service in Singapore and was able to enjoy family life at home to the full with his son and daughter.

Warships Week held during the first week of November 1941

Military and Council officials gathered on the Den bandstand at the start of Teignmouth Warships Week aiming to raise £160,000 for a Corvette War Ship. Weapons Week and Wings for Victory Weeks also received excellent local support. Teignmouth newspapers recorded a total of £119,000 being invested in Teignmouth & Shaldon's Wings for Victory Week in 1943. Investors included;

Teignmouth Electric Lighting Company - £1000
HD Gourd - £1000
Teignmouth Co-operative Society - £650
Teignmouth Quay Company - £500

The town pulled together as never before - or since. Theatrical entertainments raised funds, the Women's section of the British Legion collected materials for recycling and Teignmouth Red Cross Penny-a-Week Fund raised £1235 in one year.

Schoolchildren were encouraged to write slogans in a competition for Savings Certificates. David Markham won the first prize of a 15 shilling certificate with "They save us - why not save for them?" Other winners were

"The more you lend, the sooner the end" and one with a touch of humour "Buy planes and guns to beat the Huns".

1942

RAIDS 5
DEATHS 42
CASUALTIES 107

Facsimile copy of original records

NAME	SEX	APPROXIMATE AGE	ADDRESS	KILLED OR INJURED	RAID
TAYLOR, Percival Palmer	M		26, Gipsy Lane, Hunton Bridge, Watford, & 2, Gloucester Road.	K	2nd July, 1942. H.E.Bombs Bitton St. , Gloucester Rd. & Westbourne Terrace.
PROUT, Florence	F		1, Gloucester Road, Teignmouth.	K	do.
SMITH, Jack Thomas A.H.	C		2, do. do.	K	do.
SMITH, Dick	M		Seaman Royal Navy, 2 Gloucester Rd.	K	do.
PUCKEY, Bessie	F		1, Gloucester Rd., Teignmouth (died in hospital)	S.I.	do.
SMITH, Richard Stephen	M		2, do. do.	L.I.	do.
SMITH, Edith	F		2, do. do. (died in hospital)	S.I.	do.
SALTER, Charlotte	F		3, do. do.	L.I.	do.
WEISS, Edwin	M		"Dudleigh House", do.	S.I.	do.
TAYLOR, Ethel	F		2, Gloucester Rd. Teignmouth.	L.I.	2nd July 1942
DUNFORD, Walter	M		2, Westbourne Tce. do.	S.I.	do.
WEISS, Edwin	M		6, Albion Place, do.	S.I.	do.
BINKS, Dora	F		"West Holt", Bitton St. do.	L.I.	do.
TAYLOR, Isabel	F	12	2, Gloucester Rd. do.	L.I.	do.
WEISS, Charles	M	74	Dudleigh House, do.	L.I.	do.
CHEADLE, Florence	F	68	32, Bitton St. do.	L.I.	do.
HURFORD, Harold	M	33	3, Westbourne Tce. do.	L.I.	do.
HURFORD, Dora	F	23	do. do.	L.I.	do.
MILLS, William	M	47	32, Bitton St. do.	L.I.	do.
MILLS, Roy	M	16	do. do.	L.I.	do.
HEXTER, Frank	M	69	4, Westbourne Tce. do.	L.I.	do.
SMITH, Basil	M	32	32, Bitton St. do.	L.I.	do.

Name	Sex	Age	Address		Casualty	Date / Notes
FORD, Ada May	F	59	39, Bitton Ave.	do.	K	31st July, 1942. Two H.E.Bombs on Bitton Avenue, & The Heywoods.
CURTIS, Ida Alice	F	59	37, do.	do.	K	do.
HAMLYN, Daisy Winifred J.	F	39	41, do.	do.	K	do.
HAMLYN, Winifred Irene Sheila	C	13	41 do.	do.	K	do.
HAMLYN, Marjorie Asenath	C	9	41, do.	do.	K	do.
GOVIER, Ellen	F	86	41, do.	do.	K	do.
WHITEMAN, Edith Mary	F	50	37, Bitton Avenue, Teignmouth.		K	31st July, 1942.
WHITEMAN, Arthur	M	52	do.	do.	K	do.
WILLIAMS, Frances	F	80	55, do.	do.	L.I.	do.
WILLIAMS, Mary Ann	F	77	do.	do.	S.I.	do.
FAULKIER, Tony	C	9	1, Devonshire Place,	do.	S.I.	do.
PHARE, Evelyn	F	55	19, Coombe Vale Ave,	do.	S.I.	do.
CURTIS, Harry	M	67	37, Bitton Ave,	do.	S.I.	do.
WHITEMAN, Daphne	F	25	do.	do.	S.I.	do.
GOVIER, Lily Annie	F	80	41, do.	do.	S.I.	do.
GOVIER, Nellie	F	80	do.	do.	F.A.P. to Hospital.	do.
HOLDER, Thomas	M	66	3, The Heywoods, Teignmouth		L.I.	do.
SHARLAND, Joan Winifred	F	13	1, Glendaragh Rd.	do.	L.I.	do.
CHEESEMAN, Ada	F	55	2, The Heywoods,	do.	L.I.	do.
BAKER, Rose Ellen	F	72	1, Belgrave Terrace,	do.	L.I.	do.
CLEYDEN, Sarah	F	68	"Lyddington", Hr.Brimley,	do.	L.I.	do.
DENLEY, Lena	F	27	9, Lr.Brook St.,	do.	L.I.	do.

Facsimile copy of original records

NAME	SEX	APPROXIMATE AGE	ADDRESS	KILLED OR INJURED	PAID
BENNETT, Florence Rosina	F	38	4, Albion Place, do.	K	13th August, 1942. 8 H.E.Bombs, Albion Place, Park St. Barnpark, etc.
TAPP, Alice Maud,	F	66	7, do. do.	K	do.
CHAMINGS, Carrie	F	72	1, Barnpark Terrace, do.	K	do.
CLODE, William Wallace	M	52	4, Coombe Rd, Teignmouth.	K	13th August, 1942.
COLES, Thelma	C	6	"Isomer", Hr.Brinley, do.	K	do.
SMITH, Hazel Jacqueline	C	5	"Amberley" do. do.	K	do.
HODGE, Florence	F	53	2, Myrtle Hill, do.	K	do.
HODGE, Rose	F	51	18, Quarry Park Rd, Peverell, Plymouth.	K	do.
LEE, Alice Jane	F	66	5, Parson Street, Teignmouth.	K	do.
LOOSEMORE, Fredk.John	M	76	52A, Parson St. do.	K	do.
LOOSEMORE, Mary Maria	F	72	do. do.	K	do.
PERROW, Edward John Cook	M	63	54 do.	K	do.
COX, Eliza	F	80	9, Parson Place do.	K	do.
MORTIMORE, Maurice Louis Charles	M	26	"Sunnycrest", Bitton Hill, do.	K	do.
TAPPER, Olive Maude Pasco	F	50	53, Parson St. do.	S.I.	do.
BOYNE, Elizabeth	F	74	6, Parson Place, do.	S.I.	do.
LOCK, Thomas Francis	M	71	6 do.	S.I.	do.
ERICKSON, Frederick	M	41	5 do.	S.I.	do.
COX, Eli zabeth Ann	F	44	9 do.	S.I.	do.
NEIASS, Annie Maria	F	64	6, Albion Place do.	S.I.	do.
STACEY, Lily	F	45	3, Myrtle Hill, do.	S.I.	do.
EVANS, Ruth	F	72	do.	S.I.	do.

Facsimile copy of original records

NAME	SEX	APPROXIMATE AGE	ADDRESS	KILLED OR INJURED	RAID
BACE, GEORGE	M	39	4, Grove Avenue, Teignmouth.	S.I.	13th August, 1942 (contd)
HOOPER, Janet	C	2½	1a, Barnpark Terrace, do.	S.I.	do.
HOOPER, Emma	F	29	do. do.	Il.I.	do.
MOORE, Robert	M	12	do. do.	L.I.	do.
HATHWAY, Marjorie	F	38	Larksland, Salty Lane, Shaldon.	L.I.	do.
PRINCE, Kitty	F	3 5	3, Brimley Terrace, Teignmouth.	L.I.	do.
GIBBS, William	C	15	3, Myrtle Hill, do.	L.I.	do.
GIBBS, Henry William	M	49	do.	L.I.	do.
HODGE, William	M	50	2, do.	L.I.	do.
WHITCHER, Clara	F	79	2, Parson Street, do.	L.I.	do.
STEPHENS, Edith Elizabeth	F	44	11, do.	L.I.	do.
MITCHELL, Seth	M	77	28, Brunswick Street, do.	L.I.	do.
WATSON, Elizabeth	F	60	"Glenside", Shaldon.	L.I.	do.
PENWILL, Doreen	F	16	"Woodlands Cott: Lr.Brimley,Teignmouth.	L.I.	do.
BULLEY, Mrs.	F	59	17, Wellington Road, Exeter.	L.I.	do.
BLACKMORE, Stella	F	35	13, Lower Brimley, Teignmouth.	L.I.	do.
MINEAR, Louie	F	43	Teignmouth House, Teign St. do.	L.I.	do.
HUMPHRIES, Winnie	F	28	39, Saxe St. do.	L.I.	do.
DAPT, Percy	M	58	4, Lower Brook St. do.	L.I.	do.

Facsimile copy of original records

NAME	SEX	APPROXIMATE AGE	ADDRESS	KILLED OR INJURED	RAID
CORMODE, George	M	51	"Fairlight", Paradise Rd, Teignmouth.	L.I.	13th August, 1942. (contd)
FRIEND, Winnie	F	25	29, Mulberry St., do.	L.I.	do.
LAWREY, William	C	13	40, Willow St. do.	L.I.	do.
MITCHELL, William	M	40	40, Brunswick St. do.	L.I.	do.
THOMPSON, Constance	F	59	White Hart Hotel, do.	L.I.	do.
PRICE, Winnie	F	58	do. do.	L.I.	do.
WARNE, Donald	C	9	"Cyprus", Thornley Drive, do.	L.I.	do.
WARNE, Eva	F	19	do. do.	L.I.	do.
HARRIS, Howard	M	56	4, Wellington St. do.	L.I.	do.
BOYNE, Rosina	F	24	5, Featherstone Place, do.	L.I.	do.
BUTCHER, William	M	66	4, do.	L.I.	do.
BUTCHER, Emma	F	58	do. do.	L.I.	do.
HAYWARD, Bertha	F	60	3, do.	L.I.	do.
HAYWARD, Tercia	F	17	do. do.	L.I.	do.
CANN, Kitty	F	29	5, Albion Place, Teign St, do.	L.I.	do.
WILLIAMS, Henry John	M	82	11, Hr. Brook Street, do.	K	2nd September, 1942. Four H.E. bombs, Esplanade, Alwyns, Hr. Brook St. (2)
WILLIAMS, Elizabeth Mary	F	79	do. do.	K	do.
JAMES, Alice Jemima	F	82	do. do.	K	do.
BE ST, Florence Mary	F	73	10, do. do.	K	do.
BEST, Pauline Voran Brook	F	44	do. do.	K	do.

Facsimile copy of original records

NAME	SEX	APPROXIMATE AGE	ADDRESS	KILLED OR INJURED	PAID
GILPIN, Alice Jessie	F	68	St. Budeaux, Seymour Rd, Newton Abbot.	K	2nd September 1942 (contd)
TURPIN, Rosa Victoria	F	55	Shimpitts, Bishopsteignton.	K	do.
LOOSEMORE, Elizabeth	F	72	8, Landscore Road, Teignmouth.	K	do.
TAYLOR, William	M	33	"Hillside", Bishopsteignton.	S.I.	do.
GRAVENSTEAD, Emma	F	54	Broadlands, Shaldon.	S.I.	do.
SHARLAND, Gwendoline	F	37	"Hurley", Glendaragh Rd, Teignmouth.	L.I.	do.
NORTHWAY, Enid	F	28	Esplanade House, do.	S.I.	do.
HUBBARD, Sheila	C	3½	do.	L.I.	do.
WILLIOMBA, George	M	32	Berkeley Hotel,	L.I.	do.
BARRETT, Elsie	F		do.	L.I.	do.
BARRETT, John	M		do.	L.I.	do.
CAUSLEY, Alice	F	53	51, Brook Hill, do.	S.I.	do.
FORD, Wilfred Frank	M	43	44, Bitton Avenue, do.	L.I.	do.
TAPP, Lily	F	53	30, Bitton Avenue, do.	L.I.	do.
RENDELL, Frederick	M	41	15, Bitton Road, do.	L.I.	do.
CHAVE, Ivy	F	32	15, Northumberland Place, do.	L.I.	do.
COOK, Lewis Samuel John	M	16	14, Parson Street, do.	L.I.	do.
SMITH, Jessie	F	51	28, Exeter Road, do.	L.I.	do.
LOVERIDGE, Gwen	F	25	15, Coombe Vale Avenue, do.	L.I.	do.
SPEAR, Alfred	M	61	14, First Av., Oakhill, Dawlish	L.I.	do.

Facsimile copy of original records

NAME	SEX	APPROXIMATE AGE	ADDRESS	KILLED OR INJURED	PAID
PEATTY, J.R.		37	29, Hr. Brook St., Teignmouth.	L.I.	2nd September 1942 (contd)
SLEEMAN, Alice	F	56	23, do. do.	L.I.	do.
LAURIE, L.		29	26, Brook Hill, do.	L.I.	do.
BLACKMORE, William	M	58	15, Dagmar St., Shaldon.	L.I.	do.
FRAGALL, Fred	M	45	7, Salisbury Terrace, Teignmouth.	L.I.	do.
MOULE, Vera	F	35	6, Saxe Street, do.	L.I.	do.
MILLS, Evelyn	F	20	4, Bickfords Lane, do.	L.I.	do.
BRIDGE, W.		40	17, First Avenue, do.	L.I.	do.
CUTLIFFE, Joan	F	23	Shute Hill Crescent, do.	L.I.	do.
PADDON, Freda	C	9	2, Gladstone Terrace, do.	L.I.	do.
TAPP, Ada	F	36	30, Bitton Avenue, do.	L.I.	do.
SMITH, Fred	M	60	"Arranmore", Buckeridge Rd. do.	L.I.	do.
HAZEL, Cecil	M	57	"Rocklands", Ferndale Rd. do.	L.I.	do.
MEAD, Gladys L.	F		7, Hutchings Way, do.	L.I.	do.
BOORER, Raymond	M	15	15, Park St., do.	K	3rd November, 1942. Four H.E.Bombs, "Gwynfa", Park St. Salcombe area.
BOORER, Rhoda	F	61	do. do.	K	do.
STEVENS, Mary Alexandra	F	29	do. do.	K	
STEVENS, Ann Rhoda	F	3 months	do. do.	K	do.
YOUNG, Dora Ellen Powell	F	86	"Gwynfa Nursing Home" do.	K	do.
BOORER, Albert William	M	44	Leading Stoker, Royal Navy, do.	K	do.
GEORGE, Bessie	F	53	13, Park Street, Teignmouth.	L.I.	3rd November,1942.
SAUNDERS, Mabel	F	45	do. do.	L.I.	do.
PORTER, Eliza	F	96	"Gwynfa Nursing Home" do.	L.I.	do.
TAYLOR, Winifred	F	43	do. do.	L.I.	do.

Flight Engineer Ernest Rose DFM at Driffield, Yorkshire

Ernest Rose DFM

Teignmouth born Ernest Rose was a pupil at West Lawn School and later at the Grammar School where he joined the Air Training Corps 60 Squadron.

Ernest gained a Distinguished Flying Medal after completing 50 missions over enemy territory in Halifax Bombers with 466 & 462 Squadrons and in the Pathfinder Force where he was the only Englishman in an all Australian crew.

On D-Day 6th June 1944, Ernest witnessed the Invasion of Normandy from the air whilst flying home from operations at Chateuden Marshalling Yards in France. The historic date coincided with his 21st birthday.

After leaving the RAF he served in the Hertfordshire Police Force. Ernest died of leukaemia in 1990.

Raid 12

7th March 1942 at 9.35am   **The sea**

Machine gunning in the sea off the Pier
No casualties or damage

Two Messerschmitts (ME109s) flew in from the south east over the Pier and main streets
at a height of approximately 50 feet and opened fire with machine guns.

Raid 13

16th April 1942 at 8.05pm   **River Teign**

No High Explosives - some machine gun and cannon fire
No casualties and only minor damage

Two ME109's flew in at 50 feet from the south east and raked fishing boats, Shaldon Bridge
and Coombe Cellars with machine gun and cannon fire. Passengers on a Devon General
bus crossing the bridge were lucky to escape injury.

Raid 14

23rd April 1942 at 11.15pm   **Headway Cross and the sea**

4 High Explosives
No casualties or damage

Raid 15

Thursday 2nd July 1942 at 3.25 am   **Bitton St, Gloucester Rd**
                                               & Westbourne Terrace

3 High Explosives
4 deaths and 18 casualties
Several properties demolished and damage to forty others

An alert sounded at 1.48am. At 3.25am, a single unidentified aircraft flew in from the west at 100 feet and dropped 3 bombs on the junction of Gloucester Rd and Bitton St. Four people died, five were seriously injured and thirteen with light injuries.

Rescue and First Aid Parties were on site within 25 minutes. A Salvation Army Canteen speedily dispensed tea and hot water. Homeless people were accommodated in the temporary Rest Centre or elsewhere through the "Help Your Neighbour" scheme. Teignmouth Electric Lighting Company was praised for its swift and efficient response to complications with the electricity system. The County Controller made a site visit and immediately arranged for a party of 50 soldiers with tools and transport to clear debris from the streets.

The lower end of Gloucester Rd where numbers 2 to 5 were destroyed

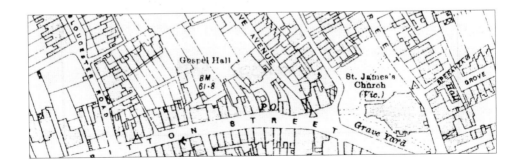

Marjorie Phillips nee Smith

Marjorie was 28 when a bomb destroyed 2 Gloucester Rd. Her mother and two brothers were killed and her father was seriously injured. He went back to light duties on the railway but died a few months later. Two younger sisters, Beryl aged 11 and 8 year old Greta went to live with Marjorie and her son of 9 in Bitton Crescent above the Hairdresser's shop run by Marjorie's husband before he joined up. His weekly RN pay of three guineas was sent back to the household that included Marjorie's blind father in law and his two daughters.

The War Office paid a weekly allowance of 13/6 (68 pence) for Beryl and Greta. Rations were as low as six ounces of meat and one egg per person a week. They all helped one another to get on with the business of surviving.

The shock of losing her family affected Marjorie very deeply. She bought nerve powders from Holman and Ham the chemist at Five Ways to help her through initially but long-term medication was the only solution. Despite this, Marjorie had a full working life and for some years was Landlady of the Prince of Wales Inn at the junction of Higher Brook St and Fore St.

Gloucester Rd

Bitton Park Rd after a raid on 2nd July 1942

This site is close to the pedestrian crossing by the Golden Lion
Avenue Terrace stands behind Oakfield on the left

Peggy Mole nee Hatherly

I was a 12 year old pupil at West Lawn School in 1942. I lived with my parents Cecil and Edie and my two year old sister at 5 Westbourne Terrace. George Symonds lived in number 1, Ern Northcott in 2, Mr Hill in 4 and Ern Shimmell in number 6. The terrace was bombed on July 2nd.

We were all together in the back bedroom when the siren sounded in the early hours. My father was in bed, mother and I on the floor beneath. As Mum grabbed my sister from her cot, a bomb exploded causing severe damage to the front of all the houses in the terrace. The first people I remember seeing were the soldiers stationed at Shaldon who raced across to help. Gloucester Rd suffered badly. Greta Smith, who later became a close friend lost her mother and two brothers.

We were covered in dust and had to go to the communal baths opposite the London Hotel in Bank St. My father went to the Council Offices at Bitton House for coupons to replace our belongings.

We moved in with my grandparents at 27 Bitton Avenue. On July 31st as I was on my way home from a swim in the sea, I heard an aircraft and went to shelter in Shaw's fish and chip shop. My grandparents' house escaped damage but three others in the Avenue were completely destroyed. Everyone had to keep silent whilst the Rescue Party listened for survivors in the rubble.

All these years later, I can still recall the smell after the raid and the sight of dead cats in the street.

Peggy (centre) and her mother (L) with holiday guests at Westbourne Terrace bombed 2nd July 1942

Gospel Hall on Bitton St

A brick built bomb shelter served this densely populated area. The row of 3-storey terraced houses survived into the 21st century

Bombed auxiliary water tank at the bottom of Gloucester Rd

Top of Parson St bombed 2nd July 1942

Almost everything was demolished except the lower pair of semi-detached houses on Mulberry St. The force of the blast tore a pair of trousers from a small boy. One person was blown from front door to back door without injury.

Pearl Trant nee Dodd

My worst fears were of being buried alive in the shelter or returning home to find all my family bombed out. We lived in Bitton St and our house was damaged in a raid. My sister Eva's bedroom was at the top of the house and an enemy plane passed the window almost close enough to touch. Eva and her friend got out just before flying debris and boulders landed on their beds. We slept downstairs in the Morrison shelter after that. When I was persuaded to go to Sunday School, there was a raid nearby and we all had to shelter.

Bombs were dropped on either side of our school at Brook Hill. It was a miracle that we were not out in the playground. Mr Whitear the headmaster of the Junior School had not blown his whistle to signal the end of lessons at the usual time because of a delay. Many of us would surely have died.

Looking west up Bitton St from the top of Parson St

A heap of lathe and plaster outside one of the numerous little shops lining the street where Bitton Park Rd flats were built in the 50s and Exeter Rd 1960s

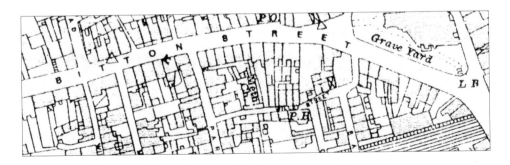

Peggy Thompson nee Skinner

In March 1942, I went to live with my two sisters at 18 Alexandra Terrace. Our husbands were away serving in the Army. Phyllis had a daughter of 11 months, Olive's son was 9 months and my own baby boy was born on July 28th with Doctor Piggott and Nurse Hellier in attendance.

Three days after Terry was born we heard enemy planes approaching at about 7pm. My sisters grabbed their babies and rushed upstairs to my room. Olive snatched Terry up from his cot and cowered in the corner beside my bed with both baby boys in her arms. Phyllis, clutching her baby girl flung herself over me on the bed. There was an almighty bang, then silence for a second. The ceiling caved in and a boulder as large as the window it came through landed on Terry's bath. The only part of the ceiling left intact was directly over my bed.

Covered in dust and debris, we managed to get downstairs and saw that the Hamlyn's house just behind us in Bitton Avenue was gone. Nurse Hellier arrived having sheltered at Shimmell's Yard in Teign St. She sent for her husband's taxi and Terry and I were carried out to it and driven to my parents home in Bishopsteignton.

The Salvation Army was wonderful! They took tea and hot water round after every raid. Neighbours helped my sisters to sort their belongings and they joined us later. Olive went to her in-laws and Phyllis stayed in our house in Fore St. There were four adults, two youngsters and two babies but we managed!

Moments before this raid, my brother Sid and sister Sheila had a lucky escape from machine gun fire down on the river bank at Bridge - our name for Luxton's Steps. Sid realized that the plane had dropped its bomb close to Alexandra Terrace and told Sheila to run home with the news whilst he raced to Teignmouth on his bike.

Soon afterwards we heard that the push had started at El Alamein. As I passed the church one afternoon, Gourd's bus pulled up and the driver, Harry Harris said he had a letter for me. It was notification from the Army that my husband Ray had been wounded. Six weeks passed before we had further news. A letter written on Red Cross notepaper arrived from Ray to say he was on the mend in a Palestine hospital. It was 18 months before he came home and saw his son for the first time.

Raid 16

Friday 31st July 1942 at 7.16 pm　　　　**Bitton Avenue, Belgrave Terrace & The Heywoods**

2 High Explosives
8 deaths and 13 casualties
4 properties demolished and 105 damaged

Two Focke Wulf 190s flew in from the north east and dropped two bombs from a height of about 300 feet. One fell 60 yards from the railway line and destroyed numbers 37, 39 and 41 Bitton Avenue. The other fell on the corner of the Railway Goods Yard damaging Belgrave Terrace and the Heywoods.

An RAF Security Boat being used by the RNAS at Haldon was attacked. Cannon and machine gun fire caused a fatality and several crew members were injured. The vessel reached its destination of Torbay under its own power.

The site of 37, 39 & 41 Bitton Avenue

Houses in the centre on Park Hill face Bitton Park

Syd Hook

On July 31st 1942, Syd was home on a 14 day Foreign Service Draft Leave. It was a perfect summer evening - still and sunny. A block wall had been built for protection at the bottom of Ivy Lane. A passageway through the barbed wire lying across the beach was kept clear for access to the River Patrol boat *Hindustan*. About a dozen Hook family members were sitting together on the sand.

At 7.15pm the siren went and less than a minute later, enemy planes came in low from the sea and headed up-river. They banked to the left about halfway up the estuary. Before disappearing over the ridge to the south of Shaldon they banked again as though they might be going towards Torbay and reappeared unexpectedly over Fuzzy Dee. Syd yelled to his family to get down. At ground level people were less of a target for shrapnel or flying masonry that could travel a considerable distance.

The planes flew one behind the other and opened cannon fire on a crowd of people raking shellfish on Salty at low tide. A bomb slid from one of the planes and ran parallel with it before nosing downwards and exploding into Bitton Avenue. Feathers from mattresses and pillows rose into the air and hung like a cloud for a long time, dimming the evening sunshine.

Hook family outside their Ivy Lane home early 1941

84

The River Patrol returned at full speed. Despite the shock of the raid, the family was able to laugh when the Hook's wire-haired terrier, Oscar sunk his teeth into Bill Boyne's trouser leg to help him off the boat and up the beach!

Meanwhile a gang of 40 dogs raced about the streets together howling like a pack of wolves. A Water Bailiff called Smith was on his way down Sun Lane when the pack overtook him and knocked him to the ground. He checked his boat on the river beach and set off back through Sun Lane. The pack, now racing in the opposite direction ran into him again and over he went for a second time!

RN River Patrol also known as Ivy Lane Navy

L-R   WH Hook : WG Matthews : WE Hook & Sport the dog : Wayne Hook
Malachi Broom : WP Boyne : W Boyne

Front   Mr Knockles (L) and Jack (Dockree) Belton both RN Engineers
Sport was drowned from *Snafell* a North Shields Minesweeper in 1941

Former sailors and fishermen formed the Royal Navy River Patrol to protect Teignmouth against invasion by sea. They installed anti-invasion tripods in the estuary and drew the boom across the river mouth each night using *Hindustan*. This was a Royal Navy requisitioned local pleasure boat *Britannia* with its name changed to avoid confusion with the RN base at Dartmouth.

Fairey Fulmar II

A Haldon based Fairey Fulmar II chased off a Messerschmitt after it bombed Teignmouth on 13th August 1942. The pilot boosted over-ride to full power but failed to catch up with the enemy aircraft as it turned for France.

The late Frank Markham commissioned Geoffery Lea to paint a Fairey Fulmar flying over the Teign Estuary. As a cadet with Teignmouth ATC 60 Squadron Frank had undertaken such a flight with a Fleet Air Arm Pilot. The painting now belongs to his brother David who kindly allowed Teignmouth Museum to reproduce it as a postcard and also its inclusion in this volume.

Raid 17

Thursday 13th August 1942 at 5.30pm   **Barnpark Terrace, Myrtle Hill Higher Brimley, Parson St, Albion Place Town Hall and Fire Station in Northumberland Place Gas Works at Broadmeadow Torquay Rd & Shaldon**

8 High Explosives including one UXB
Widespread machine gun and cannon fire
14 deaths including a Fireman and 23 casualties
16 properties demolished

Shaldon suffered its first bomb and Teignmouth experienced its worst raid to date when eight FW190s flew in from the south east at 150 feet and each dropped a bomb including the first UXB. It was previously believed that a FW190 was capable of carrying only a single 259 Kg high explosive yet the UXB was confirmed as 500 Kg by the Bomb Disposal Squad.

The town suffered from a shower of machine gunning. Two holders at the Gasworks were attacked by cannon fire causing them to burn. A pump was sent to ensure that surrounding buildings did not catch fire from the holders.

A direct hit on the Fire Station caused the death of Maurice Mortimore a young fireman. Section Leader Rowe assured the Report Centre that despite losses, capacity had been restored by sufficient replacement machines and appliances before the day was over.

Brunswick St entrance to Town Hall and Market

The gas showrooms in the corner of the building were completely wiped out. The garage to the left survived also the gabled library section on the right where public lavatories were later installed. Plans to redevelop the site have been discussed for many years.

Brunswick St filled with rubble after Teignmouth's 17th raid

Fire Station interior following the raid on 13th August 1942

Entrance to Fire Station and Town Hall from Northumberland Place

Teignmouth Electric Lighting Company's Sub Station at Shute Hill was affected by bomb blast and two transformers inside were damaged by cannon fire.

Rescue Party numbers 15 and 18 together with the Decontamination Party were split up and sent to attend the four most serious of the eight incidents.

Reinforcements came from Dawlish and Newton Abbot. Captain Kilburn who led the Barton Hall Rescue Party introduced Listening Apparatus, used for the first time, to locate casualties in Parson St. Troops from Chudleigh-based 2nd Loyals pitched in to clear the roads.

The Fleet Air Arm transported 128 homeless people to the speedily staffed Rest Centre at West Lawn Senior School where a detachment of the British Red Cross under Miss A Lynne MBE set up a Sick Bay.

The Ministry of Food Depot at Heathfield provided meals in conjunction with TUDC and the Salvation Army Canteen from Newton Abbot. The WVS also provided a canteen and distributed clothes. The Assistance Board stayed in attendance for four nights. The Rest Centre closed up again when everyone was accommodated elsewhere.

The Ministry of Information was pressed to provide a mobile broadcasting van to keep the public informed during future raids.

ARP Warden Mr J Williams was acknowledged by John Hooper in these lines to a local GP

One of the bombs fell outside the side wall of my residence and completely destroyed the building. I consider that the courage and determination shown by Mr Williams should receive official recognition as he was responsible for saving the lives of my wife and 3 year old baby. I must do all in my power to place the facts before the authorities and trust that you will be able to assist me.

I occupied the basement, ground and first floor known as 1A Barnpark Terrace. The premises, probably 100 years old were very solidly built of stone with very thick walls, the rooms large with ornamental ceilings. A bomb fell next to the end wall, the massive stonework collapsed and the building fell in. Not a wall was left standing except the one adjoining the next house and a few in the basement. At the time, I was in the centre of town. I returned to find a pile of shattered woodwork and masonry, a large crater filling with water and a tremendous escape of gas. My wife, baby, mother in law aged 70 and nephew of 12 were at the bottom with no chance of escape.

Mr Williams was directing operations. He was a total stranger to me but I have now ascertained that he has 25 years mining experience. Nothing could be heard to indicate the position of those trapped. After some time, groaning was detected and from then on he worked without rest until he had dug down nearly seven feet. Tools were passed in but he worked mostly with his bare hands.

He instructed me to lie one side and keep talking to the person located. We found that this was my wife. I kept up the conversation with great difficulty and Mr Williams continually shouted words of encouragement.

My wife complained of gas that was escaping very fast and several times she feebly stated that she could not last out. These expressions were followed each time by complete silence for a period. After nearly two hours digging, we saw a few inches of my wife's head between two very large beams that appeared to have crashed on her. Mr Williams decided it would be fatal to remove the beams if the pit was to remain open and decided to tunnel in from the outside. He succeeded in doing this after great personal effort and after dislodging several other beams and obstructions. After two more hours continuous work in a gas laden atmosphere, he released my wife and baby who was in her arms. As she was being lifted out, Mr Williams collapsed and almost fell into the hole. Later my nephew aged 12 was located and after four hours very efficient work by the official Rescue Party he was dug out. After seven hours my wife's mother was removed but she was dead.

I cannot praise too highly all those who took part. It was obvious had it not been for Mr Williams who inspired all present and led the initial operation, the result may have been very different. I feel that his actions justify the highest official recognition and I wish to do all in my power to make the facts known.

Barnpark Terrace bombed 13th August 1942

Elizabeth Higham

Mr Higham the Manager of the Gas Works and his family lived in Broadmeadow House. Elizabeth the youngest of three daughters recalls seeing trains going up the line packed with soldiers waving from the windows soon after Dunkirk. The Civil Defence dug trenches at the bottom of their garden and in the neighbouring property and banked them up with sandbags. The trenches remained for the duration but were never used. Many local people went away to escape the bombs, leaving numerous unoccupied properties in the town.

On 13th August 1942, the family had a tea party to mark Elizabeth's 13th birthday. Her two sisters and their friend who were all in their 20s decided to go to the Carlton Cinema to see "The Stars look Down". Mr Higham offered to drive them in his car but they chose to walk - a decision that saved two lives as will be revealed.

Elizabeth was helping her mother clear up in the kitchen when they heard an enemy plane. Suddenly her father shouted from the sitting room "They've got the Works!" Two large cylindrical gas holders situated close to their house had been hit by cannon and machine gun fire. Tongues of flame licked the sides and tops of the holders as Mr Higham ran down to turn off the supply. The staff plugged the bullet holes with clay to preserve the gas supply. Numerous telephone calls came through from people wanting to know if the holders were likely to explode.

Teignmouth Gas Works next to the river and railway line

If Mr Higham had driven the girls into town on that fateful day, Elizabeth would have accompanied him. Having dropped the girls at the cinema, father and daughter would have gone around the corner to the gas showrooms in the Town Hall to see what had been happening there during the day. The building received a direct hit exactly at the time they would have been inside.

Less than three weeks later with the new school term approaching, Elizabeth and her mother walked with neighbours over to Shaldon. They bought ice creams at Glenside Hotel and went to the riverside plot next to Ringmore Towers. Suddenly, enemy aircraft appeared from behind the Ness and dropped four bombs - their fins clearly visible - near the seafront. Everyone lost their ice creams as they made a dive for the bushes. Two bombs fell on Higher Brook St and another in the garden at Alwyns Nursing Home in Barnpark Rd. Esplanade Hotel was demolished by a direct hit.

An Inspector came down from London to check for structural damage at Lloyds Bank where Elizabeth's sister Evelyn worked. He found nothing significant and set off for the station. A raid occurred as he waited for the return train. As was sometimes the case, no warning was given. He returned to the Bank as white as a sheet, horrified that there had been no sirens. Evelyn told him that Teignmouth seldom got warning of air raids - they just happened!

The sand barge and Teignmouth Gas Works in the distance

West End Garage on Bitton Hill in the late 1930s

Maurice Louis Charles Mortimore of Sunnycrest on Bitton Hill on the right of the group served as a fireman in Teignmouth's NFS. During a major raid on 13th August 1942, a direct hit on the Fire Station in Northumberland Place killed 26 year old Maurice. The town was stunned by his death.

On the left is Fred Laurie, his partner in the West End Garage business.

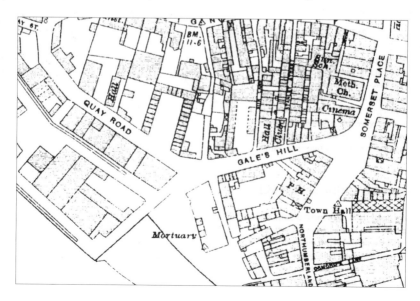

Doreen Penwill

Doreen had been to post a parcel to her brother Albert serving in the RAF and was walking along beside the Sebastopol Inn when a bomb dropped a short distance away on Myrtle Hill. The wall alongside the Inn collapsed and trapped Doreen's legs. Paddy Walsh and George Stevens dug her out from the rubble. Flying glass caused severe injuries to her leg, forehead and lower lip. The soles of her sandals were bent double.

Doctor Coldrey stitched Doreen's lip whilst Dr Courtenay held her hand. After six weeks in the temporary hospital in Hermosa Rd, Doreen and her invalid mother went to stay with relatives in London. Several pieces of glass, undetectable by X-ray were removed from Doreen at Wembley Hospital. In the years that followed, other pieces emerged through the skin.

Direct hit on 6 Myrtle Hill on 13th August 1942

June Matthews nee Stacey

Number 6 Myrtle Hill got a direct hit and was reduced to a pile of rubble. All eight occupants were brought out injured but alive. News of the raid reached Len Matthews at work as an apprentice at Morgan Giles Shipyard. He raced across the town and arrived as his future mother-in-law, Lily Stacey was being carried out. The Rescue Party kept digging to find her daughter June who was believed to be in the rubble.

In fact, June was working late in Newton Abbot and arrived home from the railway station whilst rescuers were still trying to find her.

Raid 18

Wednesday 2nd September 1942 at 4.00pm   **Seafront, Barnpark Rd**
& Higher Brook St

4 High Explosives
8 deaths and 33 casualties
5 properties demolished and damage to 160

Four FW 190s flew in from the south east at about 150 feet, each dropping a bomb. The siren could not be sounded because of damage to the electricity supply and many people were caught in the streets by machine gun and cannon fire.

Rescue Party No18, joined later by reinforcements including the Fleet Air Arm, worked for over 6 hours at the most serious incident in Higher Brook St where many people were trapped. Numbers 9, 10 and 11 were demolished and numbers 45, 46 and 47, the Victory Club and Co-op Stores were damaged. Lower down the street, numbers 21 to 27, the Drill Hall and Bird in Hand pub received significant damage. Part of the Junior School also suffered. If the raid had occurred a few minutes earlier, the pupils would have been on their way home and vulnerable to machine gun bullets or bomb fragments.

Rescue operations were hampered by huge heaps of debris in the narrow streets. Three lorries belonging to the Teignmouth & Dawlish Association of Building Trade Employees removed it. Rescuers worked on into a second day to recover the bodies of victims.

Brook Hill School
Infants and Juniors escaped with minor cuts when bombs fell on either side of the school in a daylight raid that damaged the school's windows and ceilings. Miss Best the teacher suffered severe head injuries and the loss of her mother and sister who lived on Higher Brook St.

There were 300 children on the school roll but when raids began attendance dropped dramatically. Devon County Education Committee approached the Minister of Health to arrange for the evacuation of children living on the coast. There was also the suggestion of dispersing classes in small groups across the town rather than them attending school in a single building. It was believed that the difficulties would be out-weighed by the advantages. Neither suggestion seems to have been taken up.

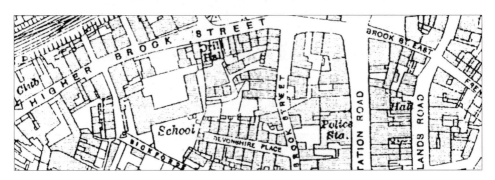

John Samuel Scown BEM

John Scown born in 1886 was the youngest Regimental Sergeant Major in the British Army during the First World War. He developed a building business in the lane bearing the family name leading off Teign St. His grandson George recalls his reply to a lady enquiring as to how business was faring - "Like a duck, madam, like a duck. All calm and serene on the surface and paddling like hell underneath!"

Scown Builders did all Shaldon's war preparation work including the gun base and pillboxes and blocking off the original Smugglers tunnel after the Army detonated the steps leading up to it from the beach. Their concrete mix was so strong that it proved almost impossible to remove in later years.

A Fire Service tower used for drying hoses was situated between Scowns Lane and the Council Yard at Gales Hill. The Royal Artillery Light Anti-Aircraft Regiment used it to mount twin Bren guns firing .303 bullets.

John Scown became Teignmouth's Rescue Party Organizer and his grandson George was messenger boy. When Exeter and Plymouth were blitzed, John's Rescue Party was called in and helped to dig out more than 60 people some of whom were members of Rescuers' own families. Their determination to free people trapped under rubble kept them working for a period of 22 hours.

John Scown was recognized with a British Empire Medal Civil Division. On Christmas Day in 1954, he lay in a coma at Teignmouth Hospital. The Salvation Army Band began to play in the hall below and John's beautiful singing voice was heard for the last time. Everyone around wept and soon afterwards he slipped peacefully away. John was, unquestionably, a local hero.

Three generations of Scowns photographed in the 1940s

John Elias (L) who served in the Royal Navy. John Henry (R) who served in the Civil Defence. In the centre is John Samuel Scown BEM who was granted the King's award for wartime service as Teignmouth's Rescue Party Organizer

Victorian elegance of 1 & 2 Esplanade

A pair of 5-storey hotels (L-R) Berkeley and Esplanade occupying the most enviable seafront position were destroyed in 1942

Esplanade Hotel bombed 2nd September 1942

Recently occupied by troops but empty at the time of the raid, it was reduced to a heap of rubble. The Berkeley Hotel was later pulled down

Brigadier Morrison's ARP Report reveals that people in the bombed areas showed remarkable fortitude and cheerfulness in spite of the ruin around them and the rain which began to fall during the evening. It included a further request:

"I would urge the provision of a mobile broadcasting van to be placed at the disposal of the Civil Defence. During last week, Teignmouth has suffered from a spate of rumours of a nature tending to upset the equanimity of the community. These rumours have been mainly concerned with gun practice and the sounding or silence of sirens. It is, at present, almost impossible to stop or refute them. A broadcasting van would have been invaluable"

RUMOURS

The Public are warned not to heed or pass on any rumours or gossip which may be heard. The truth of such rumours can always be ascertained from the Police. The law provides serious penalties for people who start or pass on rumours.

Royal Navy Rocket Projector

The gun that could be heard for miles was electrically fired and its batteries charged at Morgan Giles Shipyard

Four young Stowers with parents & grandparents in 1939

Jim (L) Eveline (2nd L) Edwin (R) and Dorcas seated (L)

Stowers Family

The family living at Vine Cottage in Heywoods Rd was greatly involved in serving King and Country. The father, John William a veteran of the First World War became an ARP warden. His wife Ethel, formerly one of Lady Astor's nurses took charge of St James Mothers' Union dedicated to raising funds to help servicemen.

The eldest son Edwin became an Admiralty Officer in Mauritius. His younger brother Jim served as a telegraphist in the Royal Navy Wireless Intelligence prior to being seconded to the 20th Indian Division in Burma. Eveline was a Theatre Sister at the Royal Devon & Exeter Hospital. Dorcas was the youngest and helped the war effort through local organizations.

In the raid on July 31st 1942, a bomb struck the gable of 1 Salisbury Terrace, bounced into a garden at Heywoods Close, rebounded over the roof of Vine Cottage and exploded at the foot of Heywoods Rd causing severe damage to all homes in the vicinity.

Touches of typical British humour shone through tragedy to lighten the darkest moments. One became a legend in the Stowers family. Ethel, a very correct lady not given to taking intoxicating liquor except in moderation at Christmas was on her way to visit a friend in Myrtle Hill. A German fighter bomber flew in over the seafront and opened fire with a machine gun. Ethel approaching the corner of French St ran for the nearest cover through the door of the Sebastopol Inn. She landed up under the counter in the arms of a well-known local character and never lived the tale down within the family circle!

Raid 19

Tuesday 3rd November 1942 at 12.50pm　　　**Railway Line west of town,
Park St, St James Church,
Coombe Rd & Reed Vale**

4 High Explosives and machine gun fire
6 deaths and 4 casualties
3 houses demolished and widespread damage to properties

Four FW 190s flew in from the direction of Newton Abbot, followed the river down past Bishopsteignton and attacked a GWR train approaching Teignmouth with machine gun fire and two bombs. One landed in the bank beside the track and the other in a field below Headway Cross. Damage to the railway line was quickly repaired.

Most of the houses between Coombe Rd and First Avenue had the majority of their windows shattered. Gwynfa Nursing Home and Thornpark School in Reed Vale were partly demolished.

Numbers 14 to 16 Park St were totally demolished by a direct hit. Fifteen other homes in the terraces of tiny cottages lining the narrow street were severely damaged and nine were later taken down. The force of the blast wrecked a Morrison shelter and blew its roof off. A young mother and her baby girl of 3 months were found dead inside it.

Park St bombed 3rd November 1942

Eight men search the rubble for survivors at the top of Park St

Four people died in Park Street that ran parallel to Fore St and about thirty yards to the west of it through the beating heart of old Teignmouth.

Warden Scown of the newly formed Light Rescue Party and Mr Pearce, Group Warden of ETN/7 were praised for their excellent work in attending to the needs of the homeless and many others and their untiring efforts often working all through the night.

In this daylight raid Anti-Aircraft Defence had only a seven second sighting yet brought down two enemy planes. Five guns expended 43 rounds of ammunition, 250 rounds of machine gun fire and 10 rounds from the seafront Rocket Projector.

Bgdr Morrison reported that:

"The latest raid, the nineteenth on the district has not impaired morale. On the contrary, the presence of AA Defence combined with the knowledge that hits were scored on an attacking plane has enhanced the already high morale of the people of this district. Fortitude and cheerfulness are dominant everywhere"

Morrison Shelters

Local fireman Harold Broom installed many Morrison shelters for domestic use helped by his young son Gordon.

The shelters were often put up in the kitchen where they were made use of as tables in the hub of the family home.

Half-inch thick steel sheet formed the roof with wire sides below. The shelters saved many lives but were not infallible.

A Ministry of Home Security Photographer recorded Harold with a buckled shelter roof.

Records of the raid on Park St state that a Morrison shelter was totally wrecked and the roof was missing.

Harold Broom with shelter roof

Joan Moyse nee Lawrey

After being bombed out of 40 Willow St on 13th August 1942, the Lawrey family was issued tickets entitling them to claim new clothes at Bitton House from a stock provided by the American Red Cross.

After being re-housed near Brook Hill School one Monday morning, another raid on Wednesday afternoon made them homeless once more. The school was damaged and part of the ceiling of the top classroom fell in where pupils including Joan sheltered beneath their desks. Miss Best the teacher was severely injured but the children escaped unhurt.

Joan believes that few people are aware of the extent of Teignmouth's wartime suffering.

Brigadier Morrison ARP Reports of 1942

These extracts show that Teignmouth still lacked adequate equipment and means of defence.

"There is distinct agitation in the district for adequate Anti-Aircraft Defence to be located in Teignmouth. The County Controller was made aware of it as soon as it was detected. The local MP has published a statement that the demand has been referred most urgently to the highest authority.

Rescue Parties cannot work properly in Battledress - they must have Overalls. Battledress is a uniform and is impractical dress for work in demolished buildings. Ankle boots offer no protection to the leg. Our people have suffered injuries due to the lack of protection above the ankle. Leather gaiters, leather knee boots or even putties are essential.

The Rescue Party went into action short of hammers, saws, wheelbarrows, pumps, lamps, axes and ladders much of which was demanded in 1938. I have furnished many lists of deficiencies in the last two years but it is still missing. Our Decontamination Party is in much the same case as regards hose. Practically, it could not function in a serious gas attack. I doubt if the effect of the lack of equipment, to which they know they are entitled, on the enthusiasm of volunteers is appreciated.

We are lucky in having a splendid body of men - mainly old soldiers and sailors - in Teignmouth. We cannot afford to let them drift away or allow their enthusiasm to wane. There is no more certain way of doing so than by the inability to supply the equipment essential for the efficient performance of the duty they have undertaken."

RAF Anti-Aircraft defence - Bren guns mounted on armoured cars

Remembered by Cartoonist Don Baker based at Shaldon 1942

Molly Nicholson

Molly Nicholson was in her late 20s when she joined the Womens' Auxiliary Air Force. Both her brothers were in the RAF and their father had served in the Royal Navy for 29 years. Public interest in Hilda Marchant a News Chronicle reporter who piloted a bomber gave rise to the idea of making a recruiting film to encourage more women to join the WAAFs, desperately needed at that time. The film was shot and Molly made a brief appearance in it.

Locals recognized her instantly and as word spread swiftly through town, the family went along to the Riviera Cinema to see her in the newsreel. Molly's son Graham recalls his mum - five foot three with a parachute on her back, walking away from a bomber where she had supposedly been at the controls. It was a memorable moment for them all.

One of two 20mm RAF Hispano Anti-Aircraft guns on Shaldon Bridge

An Hispano gun with revolving base was positioned at each end of the bridge. The area witnessed the arrival and departure of many different regiments with varying equipment particularly in the early years.

Teignmouth Open Bowls Tournament Champion for 1948 - Ken Boobyer

An encounter with a bomb in 1942 almost robbed Ken of future success

Ken Boobyer

Ken and his friend Bill were playing bowls when two planes flew over Bitton House dropping bombs close enough to damage the newly completed green. They leapt into the bushes then took shelter in the pavilion. Both escaped injury.

As a student at South Devon Technical College, Ken travelled by rail each day to Torquay and recalls a train being targeted by machine gun fire on the open stretch between Flow Point and the Gas Works. The engine tank had a couple of holes in it and carriage windows were shattered but miraculously, nobody was injured.

Ken was at work in the office of Solicitors Jordan & Kennaway on the corner of Carlton Place and George St when the appalling raid of 13th August 1942 took place. He was told to escort a female staff member home but it was difficult to find a route to Alexandra Terrace because the town was being sealed off. A bomb had fallen without exploding in the yard at the rear of Davis's Café between Northumberland Place and Brunswick St. Ken's father had come to look for him and was on the other side of the yard wall without realizing how close he was to an unexploded bomb.

A newsreel at the Carlton Cinema included footage of incendiary bombs. Later, when Ken and his mother were in the shelter at their Chelsea Place home, a commotion was heard. Ken peered through the letterbox and was amazed to see just such a bomb being defused a few feet away.

1943

Facsimile copy of original records

NAME	SEX	APPROXIMATE AGE	ADDRESS	KILLED OR INJURED	RAID
BROOK, Bernard Edward J.	M	27	8, Alexandra Terrace,	K	10th January, 1943. 5 H.E. Bombs, Powderham Terrace, Alexandra " & Central Teignmouth.
BROOK, Eileen Martha	F	27	do	do.	K	do.
BROOK, John Alexander C.	C	20 months	do.	do.	K	do.
BROOK, Edward John C.	M	19	do.	do.	K	do.
PRATT, Jessie	F	65	7, do.	do.	K	do.
PRATT, George William	M	30	do.	do.	K	do.
STEPHENS, Charles Francis	M	60	21, Saxe Street,	do.	K	do.
COUSINS, Violet May P.	F	32	16, Chapel Street,	do.	K	do.
HASTINGS, Helena	F	54	4, Powderham Terrace,	do.	K	do.
BRANCHETT, Sidney James	M	50	5, do.	do.	K	do.
CHEVERTON, Agnes Blanche	F	57	5 do.	do.	K	do.
COLEMAN, Samuel John	M	80	do.	do.	K	do.
COLEMAN, Jane Bowen Harris	F	79	do.	do.	K	do.
COLEMAN, Olive Warwick	F	54	do.	do.	K	do.
GODDARD, Florence Wilson	F	72	do.	do.	K	do.
HAMBLEY, Kate Evans	F	82	do.	do.	K	do.

Facsimile copy of original records

NAME	SEX	APPROXIMATE AGE	ADDRESS	KILLED OR INJURED	RAID
RENDELL, William Francis	M	52	5, Powderham Terrace, Teignmouth.	K	10th January, 1943
RENDELL, Peter Francis	M	17	do.	K	do.
SKINNER, Jessie	F	32	4, Hermosa Road,	K	do.
SKINNER, Herbert Lionel *	M	37	do. *P/Wtr Yo.MX.106852 H.M.S.President V" Highgate, London, N.6)	K	do.
COLEMAN, Harold	M	48	5, Powderham Terrace, Teignmouth.	S.I.	do.
RENDELL, Irene	F	50	do.	S.I.	do.
GUPPY, Dennis	C	9	"Fursey Down, HR.Woodway Rd. do.	S.I.	do.
MILLER, Samuel	M	57	4, Hermosa Road, do.	S.I.	do.
WEBB, Dennis	M	11	47, Coombe Road, do.	L.I.	do.
WEBB, Richard	M	14	do.	S.I.	do.
COLLINS, Mark	M	68	9, Bitton Street, do.	L.I.	do.
COLLINS, Ethel	F	63	do.	L.I.	do.
SHIMMEL, Frank	M	54	"Highlands", Yannon Drive,	L.I.	do.
COATES, Frederick William	M	73	11, Alexandra Terrace,	L.I.	do.
SALTER, Alfred	M	77	20, Salisbury Terrace,	L.I.	do.
STOCKER, Barbara	C	14	5, Grove Terrace,	L.I.	do.
STOCKER, Beryl	C	7	do.	L.I.	do.
SPENCE, Ann	F	66	24, Saxe Street,	L.I.	do.

Facsimile copy of original records

NAME	SEX	APPROXIMATE AGE	ADDRESS	KILLED OR INJURED	RAID
BATCOCK, John	C	9	18, Fore Street, Teignmouth.	L.I.	10th January,1943
RIDDLE, Frank	M	54	1, Coldrey Cottage, do.	L.I.	do.
RIDDLE, Minnie	F	53	do.	L.I.	do.
NEWCOMBE, Eliza	F	80	6, Speranza Grove, do.	L.I.	do.
WOOLWAY, Eliza	F	65	12, Teign Street, do.	L.I.	do.
HELLIER, Ronald	M	23	578, Battery Road, Brixham.	L.I.	do.
LEVESBY, Maurice	M	22	do.	L.I.	do.
HALLETT, Thomas	M	56	19, Saxe Street, Teignmouth.	L.I.	do.
HALLETT, Annie	F	46	do.	L.I.	do.
GEARY, Roy	C	6	39, Teign Street, do.	L.I.	do.
COLBURY, Martha	F	33	11, Alexandra Terrace, do.	L.I.	do.
CASTLE, Michael	C	8	18, Fore Street, do.	L.I.	do.
EVANS, Alice	F	74	30, Parson Street, do.	L.I.	do.

Raid 20

Sunday 10th January 1943 at 2.30pm **Powderham Terrace,**
Alexandra Terrace,
Salisbury Terrace, Bitton St,
Saxe St & Chapel St

5 High Explosives
Machine gun and cannon fire
20 dead and 27 casualties
Severe damage to numerous properties

The worst raid of the war began at 2.30pm as people cleared up after Sunday dinner. Seven FW190s came in over the sea at an exceptionally low level and fanned out. AA Defence repelled two, one of which was shot down in the sea within sight of people on the shore. The wings, part of the engine and undercarriage were later recovered. One of the retreating aircraft machine-gunned a small vessel off the coast slightly wounding two of the crew.

The other five attacked the town with machine gun and cannon fire and five bombs. Sirens sounded during the raid. It was the closest the enemy came to their target of Morgan Giles Shipyard where all the windows alongside the workshop on Strand were blown out. A fully made-up double bed landed on the roof of Big Shed causing much-needed but sardonic amusement.

Powderham Terrace numbers 4, 5 and 6 were destroyed. Most of the windows at St James Church were blown out. Severe damage occurred in Saxe St, Bitton St, Parson St and Higher Brook St.

A family of four died after a bomb hit the railway line next to the quay and bounced directly into number 8 Alexandra Terrace. The couple who lived in number 7 also died. Numbers 6, 9 and 10 were severely damaged and later pulled down.

Military assistance was invaluable in clearing the streets and bombed sites. ARP Wardens Bladon, Angliss and Bellamy were praised for their good work. Teignmouth Telephone Exchange received a mention for the cool, collected and efficient performance of their duties.

Former Mortuary
Adjacent to the Fish Quay

111

Powderham Terrace bombed 10th January 1943

The Rescue Party searches for survivors where 10 people died. High wind and the constant noise of falling debris hampered the progress of the Sound Location unit. Extraordinarily, a hen's egg survived the raid unscathed.

Saxe St bombed 10th January 1943

True Teignmothians in a tight-knit community inhabited the rows of cottages on the hill above Teign St

Barbara Skinner and Margaret Underhill nee Stocker

The sisters crouched under the sea wall when enemy aircraft appeared from behind the Ness and opened fire on the beach. Their mother kept saying "Hide your faces". It was impossible to get off the beach quickly because of anti-invasion barricades stretched along the seafront.

On Sunday 10th January 1943 the girls were off to Bishopsteignton for a birthday party. The siren went whilst they waited for the bus in Orchard Gardens and they ran to Carter's Drapery Store at the corner of Fore St where a man called Jack stood over them to shield them from flying glass. They were taken for First Aid in St James Parish Hall. Barbara was treated for shock. Margaret still has the scar from a deep cut in her leg that was dressed but not stitched.

Whilst they were there, a Mrs Woolway was brought in with her head so full of broken glass that her hair had to be shaved off. The bomb that damaged Saxe St had passed through the roof of her Teign St house. She complained that it was a bad job if the enemy disturbed her whilst she was in her own toilet!

Teign St

Twelve houses were demolished after a bomb sliced through the roof of a Teign St house, passed through several others, skidded and bounced into the air and exploded at Collins Bakery at the top of Saxe St. There were two fatalities and several casualties.

Propaganda leaflet

The public was warned "Premature notification that the war in the west has come to an end must be disregarded... We shall keep our troops at full strength and further conscription must be expected... Casualty lists will not be published.... One can count upon the intensification of British air attacks ..the Government is unable to stop this war without asking its citizens for further drastic sacrifices. We leave it to the discretion of each citizen to draw his own conclusions regarding the situation."

(The leaflet may have been produced by the British for air drops over Germany)

Collins Bakehouse at the top of Saxe St bombed 10th January 1943

Mary Collins

Just after Sunday dinner on 10th January 1943, Mary's father adjourned upstairs at the bakery in Bitton St to listen to Mr Middleton's gardening programme on the wireless. Moments later, the house was filled with the sound of loud explosions. The ceiling above the staircase began to collapse revealing the sky through a gaping hole in the roof. A woman had been killed outright by the bomb when it exploded against the bakehouse wall.

Mary who was 31 had just returned home from hospital following an operation on her knee and was far from mobile. Both parents had minor cuts to their heads so Mary was helped into the Morrison shelter in the kitchen for safety whilst they went for first aid.

A Food Office Inspector ordered that the stock of flour to be removed from the bakery and for about six months, until the business re-opened, it was stored in numerous hessian sacks in the bell tower of St James Church.

Their house was uninhabitable. A few belongings were hurriedly thrown together and they squeezed into the Exeter St home of their friends, the Hammonds. Later they moved up to Yannon Drive where two or three large guns stood in the field next to the Towers.

Mary still thinks of a woman who lost her leg when she was hit by a piece of shrapnel as she walked past the church gates. Such memories never fade and those who didn't live through it have little idea of how much everyone had to endure.

Soldiers make bombed-out buildings safe and clear the rubble in Saxe St

Willey Lane at the top of Saxe St

After Collins Bakery was bombed the site surrounding it was piled with tons of rubble from Saxe St houses, the Ring of Bells pub and Willey Lane Soup Kitchen.

Four of Greenslade's coaches were kept in the timbered garage (centre) on the site now occupied by the Alice Cross Centre. The brick store survived into the 21st century. A memorial seat marks the Bakery site at the top of Douglas House car park.

Bitton St - now Bitton Park Rd

Mrs Laurie's house at the top of Saxe St (Douglas House car park) had a direct hit whilst she was staying with her daughter Lucy at Coombe Vale Avenue opposite County Garage. Lucy tried to salvage a tea chest full of her brother's precious photographs taken all over the world but the ARP warden, Arthur Wills the Butcher forbade entry to the devastated house.

Sunday afternoon promenaders saw one of a group of Focke-Wulf 190s shot down by a pilot of a Rhodesian Squadron. The enemy aircraft crashed into the sea in the direction of Dawlish. The pilot (aged 31) who in civilian life was a gold mine manager said;

"I singled one out and gave it two long bursts and another as it re-crossed the seafront to streak for home. This last burst caused a big flash in the raider's fuselage and it went down into the sea with a tremendous splash. I was following so closely that I flew straight through the fountain of water which it threw up."

The water caused damage to the plane's radiator and front cowling but the Rhodesian flew safely back to base.

Audrey Pope nee Coleridge

The Sunday afternoon when a bomb fell on the underground water tank at the bottom of bombed-out Gloucester Rd, I was in St James Parish Hall. Some of the ceiling fell in and all the children dived for cover under the table. Bitton St was so badly damaged that we would never walk along it. Instead we ran all the way from Coombe Rd until we reached St James Church.

The day Bitton Avenue was bombed I was picking up onions at our allotment at Broadmeadow. A plane with machine guns blazing flew in low over the hedge. We had a clear view of the pilot before we threw ourselves to the ground. I remember the plane turning at the gas works.

On the night when incendiary bombs fell in Bitton Park we waited for the all-clear then went over from our house in Chelsea Place to see what had happened. It looked like fairyland to me with the trees all lit up from the fires of the incendiaries.

A bomb went through the roof of the Boyne's house at the bottom of Chelsea Place and another fell in the road. By the next morning, the bomb had been removed and the crater had been filled with earth from one of the gardens. The top of the mound had some parsley and an onion on it!

The drone of bombers was heard night after night. Just before the Avenues were bombed there was a loud whistling sound. It was very frightening and our evacuee went from the top of the staircase to the bottom in one leap.

Timber from bombed out buildings would be dumped in the streets and people used it for firewood. When some was left near our house, my brother Cyril found an oak bedhead and made it into a lovely sewing cabinet for our mother.

St James the Less Church

During a raid in 1942 a cannon shell struck the church roof causing a fire but it was rapidly brought under control. The east and south east windows were blown out. The clock on the tower had stopped at 1.50 and remained so for a considerable time.

A new east window incorporating a memorial from the original window

was made in Brighton. In 1954 the south east window was replaced. The names of 55 local men who fell in the Second World War are depicted as part of the Memorial Window. The inscription is "In sacred and grateful memory".

Alexandra Terrace and Bitton Avenue beyond

The site of numbers 6, 7, 8, 9 and 10 Alexandra Terrace. The end wall of number 5 has two newly built buttresses to reinforce it

Margaret Yandell

Alexandra Terrace where Margaret has lived all her life was bombed during the town's last raid in 1943. John Brook, a toddler of 20 months was at number 17 with his grandmother Mrs McCarthy. When it was time for dinner on that fateful Sunday, he went home to his parents in number seven. A bomb fell on the quay and bounced across the railway line directly into their house. All four occupants and the couple next door in number 8 died from injuries.

Continued…

Number 11 Alexandra Terrace and the rear of Bitton Avenue

Six people died here after the raid on 10th January 1943

Margaret's father had two lucky escapes from machine gun fire. One occurred whilst he was on duty in Teignmouth Railway Station signal box. It withstood the attack and Mr Yandell escaped injury. On a second occasion he was busy at the railway allotments at Broadmeadow when the area was sprayed with machine gun bullets.

Margaret's mother was in a booth at the Hairdressers in Bitton St when a bomb dropped nearby and everything suddenly went black. After the all-clear, she hurried back to a neighbour's house to collect Margaret. The lady, who was still inside the Morrison shelter called out "Mrs Yandell, please take my cakes out of the oven - they'll be burnt!"

Raid 21

Tuesday 18th May 1943 at 2.45am   **Bitton House & Park**
                                            Shaldon

2 High Explosives and 216 Incendiary bombs
No deaths or injuries
Damage to Bitton House and Teign House Hotel at Shaldon

A single twin engine bomber flying very low made a night raid. It was the only experience of incendiary bombs in the district. An estimated 216 fell but 101 of the one Kilo bombs dated 1937 did not function. Four fell on the upper floor of Bitton House causing small fires that were quickly brought under control by women Fire Auxiliaries on duty in the premises.

A ring of incendiaries surrounded Bitton House and others fell on the bowling green. Three more fell on the Isolation Hospital causing a fire in the mortuary. Bitton Court was developed on the site of the Isolation Hospital in the 1980s.

A high explosive fell in the river 30 to 40 yards out from the south bank. A second fell 20 yards away destroying the east wing of Teign House Hotel next to St Peter's Church. The front of the hotel caved in through the blast.

United States Navy

In 1943 the shipyard acquired new neighbours when the US Navy established a workshop beside Lifeboat Lane and installed four service bays and a turntable.

The ferry landing currently in use was established about 1942. The former hauling-up slip across the river beach was closer to the Point and the US Navy made use of it to bring in Landing Craft for service. Boat crews trained here before going on to Slapton Sands to rehearse for the Normandy landings of June 1944.

The US Navy's superior equipment made a significant impact and helped to turn the tide of war in the Allies' favour. Their support lifted spirits and boosted morale. Some local girls enjoyed the novelty of dancing with men who talked like film stars but others would only partner "our boys".

They departed from Teignmouth with a typically facetious gesture. At a pre-arranged signal, all the billet windows along the seafront opened and numerous "balloons" - inflated condoms - were released on the Den.

Harry Sealey

Harry was apprenticed to Morgan Giles Shipyard in 1937 when fully fledged journeyman boat builders got £3.8s and labourers £2.10s for a 47 hour week. He earned five shillings a week and 2d per hour overtime. War caused dramatic changes to the yard. Harry was forced to grow up very fast and at 17 his boss told him to lay down a keel for a 35 foot naval pinnace.

He was soon put in charge with people working under him. The workforce built motor torpedo boats, landing craft, motor and harbour launches and those used for air and sea rescue. They also built a lifeboat. Half the yard was dedicated to repairs and those involved with building were often called to the repair side.

Harry aged 24 at Morgan Giles Shipyard in 1947 when Admiralty work was still being carried out

Each Tuesday and Thursday evening and Sunday morning Harry donned his Home Guard uniform and went for drill practice. Every fifth night, the unit patrolled on Haldon. The arrival of the US Navy in 1943 provided a much-needed boost to morale and invaluable support. They installed a turntable and re-fit bays in the car park in front of Lifeboat House. A control panel for observing and signalling was put on the roof of the Marina Hotel.

Americans were always keen to trade. One of them visited all the billets along the seafront and bought anything service men wanted to exchange for cash. Cigars, cigarettes, boots of unstained leather and heavy-duty overalls were bargained over in quiet moments at the yard. Harry bought some overalls and paid only two shillings because there was a huge yellow letter P on the back - USA Prison Issue! He painted over the letter and they lasted years!

As D-Day approached Harry was told that within three weeks he'd be in the Navy as a PO. His call-up papers did not come. Later he was warned to have his toolbox ready to take across to France. He's still waiting further orders!

River Beach and Harbour in 1943 as remembered by Harry Sealey

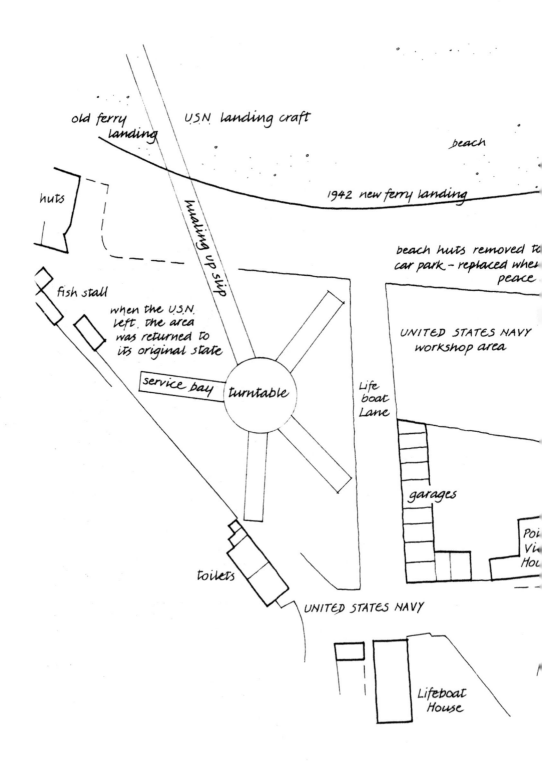

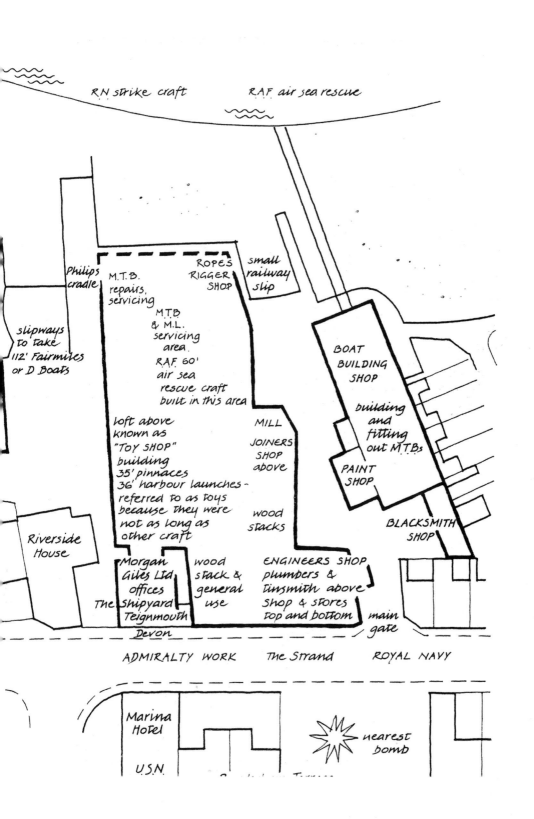

RN strike craft   RAF air sea rescue

Philips cradle

slipways
to take
112' Fairmiles
or D Boats

M.T.B. repairs, servicing

ROPES RIGGER SHOP

small railway slip

M.T.B & M.L. servicing area.

R.A.F. 60' air sea rescue craft built in this area

BOAT BUILDING SHOP

building and fitting out M.T.Bs

loft above known as "TOY SHOP" building 35' pinnaces 36' harbour launches - referred to as toys because they were not as long as other craft

MILL

JOINERS SHOP above

PAINT SHOP

wood stacks

Riverside House

Morgan Giles Ltd offices

wood stack & general use

ENGINEERS SHOP plumbers & tinsmith above Shop & stores top and bottom

BLACKSMITH SHOP

The Shipyard Teignmouth Devon

main gate

ADMIRALTY WORK   The Strand   ROYAL NAVY

Marina Hotel

nearest bomb

U.S.N.

River Beach and Harbour in 1943 as remembered by Harry Sealey

two Hispano guns
R.A.F. Regiment

MC

U.S.

Plans drawn by Bill Barter

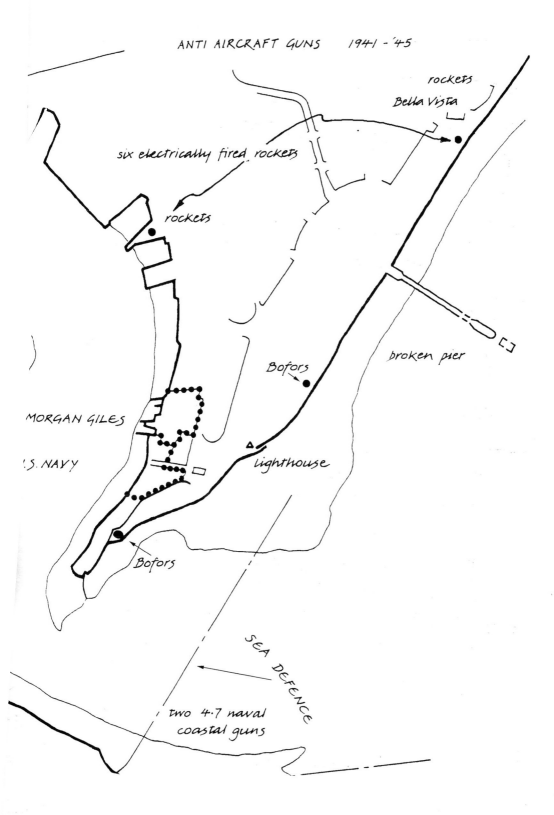

ANTI AIRCRAFT GUNS   1941 - '45

rockets
Bella Vista

six electrically fired rockets

rockets

broken pier

Bofors

MORGAN GILES

'S. NAVY

lighthouse

Bofors

SEA DEFENCE

two 4.7 naval
coastal guns

Cyril Carr

In 1943 Cyril, a Suffolk man arrived in Teignmouth as a 21 year old Leading Aircraft man. Posted from Dorset he was part of a 40-strong RAF Squadron Number 2892. His billet was Seacroft Hotel on the seafront, others were at Gregson's in Station Rd. Less fortunate were those billeted in Shaldon's Victoria Hall.

The most recent raid on Teignmouth since his arrival proved to be the final one involving loss of life. Duty hours were four on and four off for the Squadron with the sole task of providing round the clock Anti-Aircraft Defence with 20mm Hispano guns on revolving bases.

Two were placed on the seafront - one by the underground toilets and the other near the lighthouse. A third at the seaward end of the Pier was reached by walking planks placed over voids where sections had been removed to prevent invaders. Other guns were placed at the top of Exeter Rd close to Rocky Lane, Buckeridge Rd allotments, on top of the bombed Hospital at Mill Lane and two on Shaldon Bridge.

Compared to a posting on the Kent coast beset by doodle-bug raids, Cyril found Teignmouth a quiet backwater and took it immediately to heart. On their weekly day off, the airmen enjoyed the company of local young ladies. Cyril fell for Pearl Sampson who showed her devotion by riding a bicycle out to Moretonhampstead to visit Cyril recovering from concussion in the makeshift hospital at GWR Hotel. He had slipped on a tablet of soap after Sunday morning ablutions at Seacroft and fallen down the entire length of the staircase. Pearl's war effort was in assisting riveters constructing MTBs at Morgan Giles Shipyard.

One Sunday afternoon a spiral of smoke was seen above Babbacombe. A church had been bombed by enemy aircraft that dodged fire from gun crews sited along the cliffs between Torbay and the Ness. Cpl Colley fired from the end of the Pier, hit the plane's underside and it crashed seven miles out.

In May 1944 Cyril and Pearl were married and settled into a life of contentment bringing up their family in Teignmouth.

1944

FINAL RAID - NO LOSSES OR INJURIES

1945

VICTORY YEAR

Raid 22 - the final one

Monday 29th May 1944 at 1.40am   **Bishopsteignton**
Little Haldon Rd

8 High Explosives including 1 UXB dropped on open ground
No deaths or casualties
Slight damage to property in Bishopsteignton

The road 300 yards west of Gipsy Corner was blocked when a 1000Kg UXB exploded in a nearby field. The road was closed for five days and the RNAS based at Bishopsteignton used an alternative route to the Aerodrome.

Holcombe Head - Derncleugh House and garden on the left

During the last year of the war, 16 year old Alan Paul from Salcombe worked in the walled garden of Derncleugh House at Holcombe. Most of the 3 acres were given over to food production but it was permissible to grow violets in ten per cent of the ground.

There were several violet growers in the vicinity. The variety favoured at Derncleugh was named after the Princess of Wales who became Queen Alexandra. It was large with a wonderful perfume. At Christmas a single bloom would make tuppence. The violet season stretched from late autumn through to the spring. Each morning the violets were picked and bunched. In the afternoon they were boxed and driven down to Dawlish Railway Station. Early the following morning, the violets were wholesaled at Covent Garden. Sellers at stations and street corners in London charged about two shillings for a bunch of two dozen. Violets were always popular - one breath of their perfume and you were back home in Devon!

203 Devon Home Guard

When France fell in 1940, Colonel Colin McVean Gubbins set up a secret army of civilians to defend this country in the event of invasion. Battalion 203 covered the south coast. Devon had 140 members in teams of 5 or 6 who were the first men to be issued with Tommy guns, plastic explosives, cyanide pills and sticky bombs that could cling to a tank and penetrate inch-thick armour on explosion. They constructed a series of hide-outs 20 feet below ground and filled them with supply stores and arms. One was unearthed in recent years during major construction on Telegraph Hill.

On 19th November 1944 a Stand Down was ordered. The existence of such Auxiliary Units had been confidential information therefore the men received no acknowledgement of their service to King and Country. In the year 2000 a Defence Medal was posthumously awarded to Cecil Hatherly, second from the right in the back row.

The Stand Down in 1944 possibly at Ashcombe Woods

Combined Unit of Royal Navy, Royal Marines & Royal Air Force 1945

At the Courtenay Hotel where plans for the Normandy Invasion were laid

David Nicholson

From 1943-45, David was with HMS Mount Stewart, a shore establishment named after two Commanders who developed the combined unit of Royal Navy, Royal Marines and Army specializing in irregular warfare.

Captain J Brunton RN commanded the unit of 25 WRNS, 60 ratings and 35 officers operating from Eastern Dock and garages on Lifeboat Lane. Three types of specialized craft were developed and tested in local waters.

1. EMBs - Explosive Motor Boats of 12 foot length. Dropped with a driver aboard with three parachutes from Lancaster bombers. The helm was locked on towards its target and the driver returned to safety by any means open to him.

2. MSCs - Mobile Submersible Canoes, electrically-operated rigid canoes about 9 foot long. The driver wore a diving suit in the craft that moved through the water like a porpoise. MSCs worked in conjunction with :

3. MFUs - Mobile Flotation Units - part submarine and part surface craft with diesel engines. Two models were used, one 29 foot and the other 59 foot length. The crew of three submerged the MFU then, under cover of darkness used two canoes to set limpet mines on German ships. An infra-red lamp guided the crew back to the MFU, brought to the surface by a time clock.

The unit used the Royal Hotel and had Glendaragh Hotel as a Wardroom. They underwent diving courses from the end of the Pier and, David says, had lots of fun!

Peter Lewis

Royal Marine Peter Lewis is the last one right in a khaki shirt, second row in the group photograph opposite. The Marines, billeted at the Courtenay Hotel had a rigorous training programme. Equipment was tested on the sea bed by teams of ten divers. Cliff climbing was practiced above Smugglers beach reached by motor boat. Periodically they went out to sound the Bar and ascertain water levels using a local barge.

The main HQ for the combined unit was at Riverside opposite Lifeboat House. Marina Hotel was a Royal Navy and Fleet Air Arm billet and the Mess and Sick Bay were based at Overcliff on Dawlish Rd.

Peter was on LCF20, the fourth landing craft to reach the French coast for the Normandy landings. His 20th birthday fell on 6th June 1944 but to Peter's chagrin, he missed his tot of rum due to such extreme circumstances!

Soon after the photograph in 1945, Peter's unit loaded stores at Plymouth and prepared for the Far East to destroy steel submarine nets blocking harbours. Victory in Japan was declared and the Marines were called off. Peter went to Chatham, returning in 1946 to marry his sweetheart, Cynthia Mortimore.

Nissen huts in the garden of Courtenay Hotel

On VE Day, Royal Marines used redundant telegraph poles for a bonfire outside the Courtenay. The tarmac melted giving rise to strong comments!

133

Louisa James Diary Extracts during April and May 1945

Louisa was the wife of Revd Francis B James, Superintendent Minister of Teignmouth Methodist Church 1944-48. Their son Martin became Minister there in the 1990s.

Mon April 30th   Amazing news keeps coming through.

Tues May 1st   Put Forces news bulletin on at 11am and the first thing heard was Hitler is dead. Stayed up till midnight to see if further news came through. It did, saying he had been killed at his post in Berlin. A new man has taken his place who says he is going to carry on. This is not defeat.

Weds May 2nd   Reports now say that Hitler committed suicide - and Goebbels. What is one to believe? German armies in Italy have surrendered unconditionally.

Thurs May 3rd   Hamburg surrendered now-there is little left.

Fri May 4th   News at 8am seems to indicate that the end is near. All is very unsettling and work seems impossible.

Sat May 5th   Listened all day for Peace news but it did not come.

Sun May 6th   Feeling very unsettled. Peace is in the air and Germany is surrendering.

Mon May 7th   Very tense sort of day. Expecting news. Each hour the announcer said it was very near then about 7.30pm, they said it would be given at 3pm tomorrow. Town all decorated-feeling of excitement. What a day! Though not officially given, the European war is over. Six years nearly.

Tues May 8th   Listened to Mr Churchill make the great announcement. All went out afterwards to look at the decorations. Crowds of people about. Went to Church for our own service of thanksgiving. It was full downstairs-a very beautiful service. Then got supper and listened to the King. He was quite good but it is painful to listen to him. Other broadcasts included Field Marshall Montgomery. He was so simple and so good and struck a real Christian note. At 11pm the town was very seemly and quiet. Listening to London, it is more lively there. Can you blame them? But Oh the relief, sense of security and no fear of sirens. What years! How good God has been- all of us spared. May we be worthy of such kindness and mercy.

Weds May 9th   Went to Service on the Den at 3pm. What a crowd and quite good service. Frank read the lesson. Later listened to tribute to Churchill. Very, very interesting especially to hear his war speeches - they were really very good.

Thurs May 10th   Our blackout is not yet lifted, afraid of submarines. Petrol ration to be increased-the first restriction.

Fri May 11th   Heard the blackout has been rescinded at last. Oh what joy after 6 years! Got the paper off the lounge windows also some blackout curtains down.

Pat Penwill nee Brown

But for the fact that Mum and I waited for our cat to come in before we went out, we would have been on the seafront when the pier was bombed in July 1940. We left our home above Burton's Stores in Bank St in August 1942 because of an unexploded bomb in the yard of Davis Café, next to the bombed out Market Hall. We took our two evacuees and went to live with friends in Yannon Terrace.

I didn't like West Lawn School's air raid shelter. If the siren sounded, I ran up Exeter Rd to be with my Mum and on the first note of the all-clear, scampered back to catch up with my friends returning to the classroom. The teacher never found out but I realised later that it was wrong in case the need for a head count had arisen.

I was at St Michael's Sunday School during a raid. We got under the pews then moved into the bell tower. The thought that the stonework might fall on us was very frightening. Smoke and rising dust obliterated Mum's view of the tower from Yannon Terrace and she feared the church had been bombed.

Over the years, twelve evacuees from various places stayed with us. We had happy times together, putting on concerts in our sitting room to entertain the grown-ups. I am still in touch with some of them. Albert and I were pleased that one was able to attend our Ruby Anniversary celebration in 1999.

The Bandstand on VE Day

Town Youth Club members including Bill Webber, Gillian Sampson,
Clifford Taylor, Mary Stephens, Pat Brown, Jack Mortimore, John Sleeman,
George Scown, Valerie Knight, Peter Crispin, Diana Hexter, Stephanie Beatty,
Jean Ford, Hilary Phillips and Pam Stacey

Pauline Seaton nee Rose

Every waking moment was occupied during wartime. Pauline joined the Girls Training Corps based at West Lawn School and learned first aid, aircraft identification and Morse Code. Less exciting but essential sessions of Make Do and Mend inspired novel recycling of items in short supply. There was no time for teenage blues or boredom!

Pauline went fire-watching from the rooftops above Den Rd, did overnight duty at the Report Centre in the basement of Bitton House and was sent into a smoke-filled hut in Bitton Park during Civil Defence training.

She joined the staff at Barclay's Bank where each week they had to work for a while wearing gas masks. It only took place after the Bank closed its doors to the public and invariably caused much hilarity!

Each time she returned home to Shute Hill, Pauline would pause at the front gate. If the wireless was playing she knew that all was well. The safety of her fighter pilot brother Ernest was paramount. The sound of the wireless confirmed that no dreaded telegram had arrived.

GTC in Railway Station Yard for Parade to mark Victory in Europe
Two days of official celebration took place - this was VE plus 1

L-R   Officer Matthews : Georgina Stephens : Joan Fragall : Pauline Rose
J Bryant : Jean Churchill : Nancy Broom : Audrey Churchill
Gwen Hayman : Rene Matthews : Eva Dodd : Mary Helmore
Beryl Cook : Doreen Knapman : Officer Groves

Victory Parade led by the Royal Navy

Thanksgiving for Victory!

Teignmouth's outburst of thanksgiving was best illustrated by the attendance of 8-9000 people who gathered on the Den for a United Service on 9th May 1945.

Most of the town's organizations assembled in Station Yard and marched to the Den headed by the Teign Battalion Cadet Band where they were joined by the Brownies and pupils from the Junior School and their greatly respected Headmaster, Mr JC Whitear.

Loud applause greeted the British and American Navy and Marines as they marched past the 13 flags of the Allies mounted by the Bandstand.

Involved in the Victory Parade were;
Royal Navy, Royal Marines, WRNS and US Navy
National Fire Service, Coastguards, Sea Cadet Corps,
Devon Army Cadets
King's Royal Rifle Corps Cadets (Haberdasher Aske's School)
Air Training Corps, Girls' Training Corps, Sea Rangers
Hospital Matron & Nurses
Home Guard, British Legion, VAD, Civil Defence,
Womens Voluntary Service, Townswomens' Guild, Mothers' Unions of
St James and St Michael's, Girl Guides, Boy Scouts and Cubs

Thanksgiving Service conducted from Den Bandstand

A crowd estimated as 8-9000 gathered on the Den for the service led by six local clergymen. The Salvation Army Band accompanied the singing led by church choirs and conducted by Mr Jack Price. It closed with the National Anthem and a gramophone record of The Star Spangled Banner

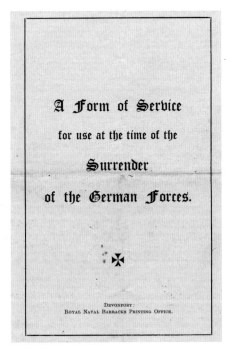

A crowd of 8-9000 people gathered on the Den for the Thanksgiving Service

Bank St hangs the flags out for Victory in Europe on 8th May 1945

SH Doel outlived neighbouring businesses and reached the 21st century

Street Parties for Victory!

Saxe St had a tea party and sing-song for residents and 70 children

**Nell Tibbs and (L-R) Robin, Janet and Brian
at First Avenue's Party for 76 children**

Teign View Place where adults out-numbered children

Third Avenue residents celebrate Peace

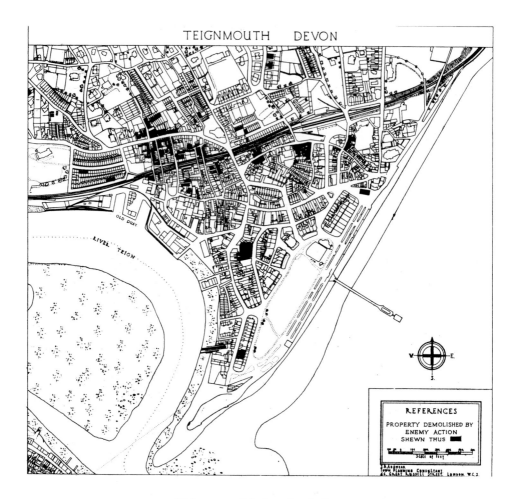

Teignmouth's bombed sites

COUNTING THE COST ON A LOCAL SCALE

July 1940 to May 1944

Teignmouth, Shaldon and Bishopsteignton endured

ALERTS	460
AIR ATTACKS	22
HIGH EXPLOSIVES	79
INCENDIARIES	1000
DEATH TOLL	79
CASUALTIES	151
HOUSES DESTROYED	228
HOUSES DAMAGED	2250

PROPERTIES DELETED FROM VALUATION LIST ON ACCOUNT OF WAR DAMAGE

Date of Proposal	Asst. No.	Situation of Property	OLD Gross.	R.V.	As now Amended Gross.	R.
			£.	£.	£.	£
3. 2. 42.	1538	Kingsdown, Linfield	48	38	-	-
	1539	" Heswall	30	22	-	-
	1778	25, Mulberry St.	7	4	-	-
	2424	43, Second Avenue	21	14	-	-
	2426	45, " "	21	14	-	-
	2428	47, " "	21	14	-	-
	2430	49, " "	21	14	-	-
1. 9. 42	5	5, Albion Place	9	5	-	-
	6	6, " "	9	5	-	-
	7	7, " "	11	7	-	-
	100	1, Barnpark Terrace	70	56	-	-
	206	35, Bitton Avenue	20	12	-	-
	8	37, " "	22	15	-	-
	210	39, " "	20	12	-	-
	212	41, " "	20	12	-	-
	305	23, " Street	30	22	-	-
	306	24, " "	16	10	-	-
	307	24a, " " (shop)	20	12	-	-
	315	32, " "	30	22	-	-
	3030	33, " " "	18	11	-	-
	3031	33a, " " "	15	9	-	-
	317	33b, " " " "	20	12	-	-
	329	43 " "	40	30	-	-
	330	44 " "	32	24	-	-
	331	45 " "	35	26	-	-
	332	46 " "	30	22	-	-
	333	47 " "	16	10	-	-
	334	47a " "	18	11	-	-
	336	49 " "	32	24	-	-
	337	" "(Advert Sign)	-	1	-	-
	338	49a " "	10	6	-	-
	339	50 " "	28	21	-	-
	340	51 " "	25	18	-	-
	1	52 " "	25	18	-	-
	2	53 " "	28	21	-	-
	3	54 " "	26	19	-	-
	4	" " (Advert Sign)	-	1	-	-
	5	55 " "	27	20	-	-
	6	56 " "	30	22	-	-
	7	57 " "	27	20	-	-
	393	6 Brimley Villas	50	40	-	-
	394	7 " "	35	26	-	-
	416	Brunswick St.Burdicks Gge.	70	56	-	-
	502	Chapel Street (Store)	15	9	-	-
	1187	2, Gloucester Road	18	11	-	-
	1188	3, " "	28	21	-	-
	1189	4, " "	24	17	-	-
	1190	5, " "	24	17	-	-
	1789	2, Myrtle Hill	28	21	-	-
	1790	3, " "	32	24	-	-
	1791	4, " "	11	7	-	-
	1792	5, " "	12	7	-	-
	1793	6, " "	26	19	-	-
	2082	5, Parson Place	10	6	-	-
	3	6, " "	10	6	-	-
	4	7, " "	10	6	-	-
	5	8, " "	12	7	-	-
	6	9, " "	12	7	-	-
	7	10, " "	12	7	-	-

Date of Proposal	Ass. No.	Situation of Property	OLD Gross. R.V.		AS NOW Amended Gross. R.V.	
1. 9. 42.	2090	1,Parson Street	9	5		
	1	2, " "	9	5		
	2	2a, " "	7	4		
	2132	52 " "	16	10		
	2133	52a, " "	14	8		
	2134	53 " "	14	8		
	2135	54 " "	14	8		
	2739	1, Westbourne Terrace	20	12		
	2740	2, " "	20	12		
	1	3, " "	20	12		
	2	4, " "	20	12		
	3	5, " "	20	12		
	4	6, " "	20	12		
	417	Town Hall etc.	80	64		
	418	" " Store	25	18		
	419	" " "	15	9		
	420	" " "	65	52		
	1	" " "	10	6		
	2	" " "	6	4		
	3	" " "	12	7		
	4	" " "	6	4		
	5	" " "	6	4		
2. 3. 43.	14	6, Alexandra Terrace	18	11		
	15	7, " "	18	11		
	16	8, " "	18	11		
	17	9, " "	18	11		
	18	10, " "	18	11		
	304	22, Bitton Street	30	22		
	308	25, " "	18	11		
	309	26, " "	22	15		
	310	27, " "	35	26		
	311	27a, " "	50	40		
	318	34, " "Office & Str.	15	9		
	319	35, " "	26	19		
	335	48, " "	30	22		
	392	5,Brimley Villa	45	35		
	395	8, " "	35	26		
	506	15,Chapel Street	13	8		
	778	37,Daimonds Lane	14	8		
	779	38, " "	14	8		
	919	11, Devonshire Place	11	7		
	920	12, " "	11	7		
	921	13, " "	11	7		
	922	14, " "	11	7		
	934	2, Esplanade	130	105		
	935	1, Esplanade	130	105		
	1140	1, French Street	23	16		
	1230	11, Grove Avenue	18	11		
	1411	9, Higher Brook Street	25	18		
	1412	10, " " "	24	17		
	1413	11, " " "	35	26		
	1414	12, " " "	95	76		
	1423	18, " " "	22	15		
	1424	21, " " "	8	5		
	1425	22, " " "	11	7		
	1426	23, " " "	11	7		
	1427	24, " " "	7	4		
	1428	25, " " "	10	6		
	1429	26, " " "	10	6		
	1450	47, " " "	31	23		
	1483	9, Hollands Road (shop)	10	6		
	1517	1, Indus Cottages	9	5		
	1518	2, " "	9	5		
	1519	3, " "	9	5		
	1674	10, Lower Brook Street	12	7		

Date of Proposal	Asst. No.	Situation of Property	OLD Gross. R.V.		As now Amended Gross. R.V.	
2. 3. 43.	1675	11, Lower Brook Street	11	7		
	1678	2, The Court -do-	10	6		
	1679	3, " " -do-	10	6		
	1680	4, " " -do-	10	6		
	1681	5, " " -do-	10	6		
	1682	6, " " -do-	10	6		
	1683	Bird-in-hand -do-	60	48		
	1684	15, Lower Brook Street	10	6		
	1685	16, " " "	20	12		
	1767	8, Mulberry Street	13	8		
	1768	9, " "	13	8		
	1769	10, " "	12	7		
	1777	24, " "	8	5		
	1783	30, " "	25	18		
	1784	34, " "	18	11		
	1785	35, " "	11	7		
	1786	36, " "	11	7		
	1788	1, Myrtle Hill	25	18		
	1844	Market House	11	7		
	1983	2, Old Quay Street	11	7		
	2017	Osmond Lane (Store)	8	5		
	2058	6, Park Street	12	7		
	2059	7, " "	12	7		
	2060	8, " "	12	7		
	2061	9, " "	10	6		
	2062	9A, " "	10	6		
	2063	10, " "	10	6		
	2066	13, " "	18	11		
	2067	14, " "	18	11		
	2068	15, " "	19	12		
	2081	4, Parson Place	10	6		
	2088	11, " "	12	7		
	2089	12, " "	12	7		
	2128	48, " St.	14	8		
	2129	49, " "	14	8		
	2130	50, " "	14	8		
	2131	51, " "	14	8		
	2192	4, Powderham Terrace	65	52		
	2193	5, " "	65	52		
	2194	6, " "	65	52		
	2221	Thornpark School, Reed Vale	45	35		
	2222	Gwynfa	50	40		
	2340	18, Salisbury Terrace	24	17		
	2341	19, " "	26	19		
	2362	16, Saxe Street	10	6		
	2363	17, " "	11	7		
	2364	18, " "	10	6		
	2365	19, " "	10	6		
	2366	20, " "	11	7		
	2367	21, " "	13	8		
	2368	22/23 " "	26	19		
	2369	24 " "	15	9		
	2370	25 " "	15	9		
	2371	26 " "	18	11		
	2372	27 " "	18	11		
	2485	4, Speranza Grove	16	10		
	6	5, " "	16	10		
	7	6, " "	16	10		
	8	7, " "	16	10		
	9	8, " "	16	10		
	2578	19, Teign Street	10	6		
	9	20, " "	10	6		
	2630	2, Terra Nova Place	10	6		

Date of Proposal	Asst. No.	Situation of Property	OLD Gross	R.V.	As now Amended Gross	R.V.
2. 3. 43.	2761	4, Willey Lane	12	7		
	2762	5, " "	12	7		
	2763	6, " "	12	7		
	2764	7, " "	12	7		
	2768	12/13 " "	16	10		
	2769	16/17 " "	18	11		
	2772	Ring of Bells Willey Lane	48	38		
	2773	Soup Kitchen " "(Store)	2	1		
	2766	14, Willow Street	9	5		
	7	15, " "	9	5		
	8	16, " "	9	5		
	9	17, " "	8	5		
	2798	33, " "	24	17		
	2799	34, " "	17	10		
	2800	38, " "	10	6		
	2801	39, " "	10	6		
	2802	40, " "	10	6		
	2863	Bitton Street, House, (Elect.Co.) L-up-shop Offices etc.	40	30		
	3176	Higher Brook St. Victory Club	35	26		
	3177	46a, " "	17	10		
	3181	8, Old Quay St.	9	5		
	2	do.	9	5		
	3	do.	9	5		
21.9. 43	2765	8, Willey Lane	11	7		
	6	9, " "	11	7		
	2767	10, " "	11	7		
	2771	18, " "	11	7		
	2919	Yannon Drive, Peribank	28	21		
5. 9. 44	546	12, Commercial Road	19	12		
	1432	28/29,Higher Brook St.	25	18		
	2052	1, Park Street	12	7		
	1761	2, Mulberry Street	14	8		
	1762	3, " "	14	8		
	2097	7, Parson Street	18	11		
	8	8, " "	9	5		
	9	9, " "	8	5		
	2100	10, " "	14	8		
	1	11, " "	10	6		
	2	11A, " "	10	6		
	2127	47 " "	20	12		
	2776	4, Willow Street	12	7		
	7	5, " "	12	7		
	8	6, " "	12	7		
	9	7, " "	12	7		
	2780	8, " "	12	7		
	1	9, " "	12	7		

3266

TO 30. 9. 44. = Houses 212
Shops
&c. 21

146

PROPERTIES REDUCED IN VALUE ON ACCOUNT OF WAR DAMAGE &C.

Date of Proposal	Asst. No.	Situation of Property	Reasons for Reduction	Odd G.V.	R.V.	New G.V.	R.V.
2. 3. 43	388	1, Brimley Villas	Garage destroyed	56	45	50	40
	929	1, Eastbrook St.	House damaged	28	21	23	16
	964	1, Exeter Street	Store etc. destroyed	55	44	50	40
	1345	Heywoods Bungalow	do.	30	22	25	18
	1677	13, Lower Brook St.	Bakehouse destroyed	28	21	23	16
	2220	Greenbank, Reed Vale.	Partially damaged	60	48	40	30
	2864	Chapel Street	Store Demolished	9	5	1	1
	76	Barnpark Rd.-Avila	Damaged & used as Store	40	30	32	24
	2227	Reed Vale,-The Moorings	Garage destroyed	50	40	45	35
	2254	25, Regent Street	Partial War Damage	45	35	35	26
		T & S. Bridge		2630		735	
				2941		981	

S H A L D O N

21. 9.43	47	Teignbridge House	Partially demolished	140	113	115	90
				3054		1071	
				1071			
				1983			
				3266			
			LOSS in R.V.	£ 5249 to 30.9.44.			

Lucky Escapes

Joan Squire

Joan left Teignmouth on a Devon General single decker bus to travel home to Torquay (16.4.42). She sat in the corner of the long back seat and as the bus crossed over the bridge to Shaldon at around 8pm, an enemy plane was spotted coming in from the sea. It opened fire with its machine gun.

The driver put his foot down and did not stop until he reached St Peter's Church. The driver and conductor got off to inspect the rear corner of the vehicle below Joan's seat and beckoned to her.

It was a shock for Joan to see the huge hole the bullets had torn in the bodywork only inches away from her. The passengers had a whip-round to reward the driver for his quick wits.

Reg Matthews

When the Town Hall was bombed, a large piece of flying masonry landed four feet away from Reg who was on the back beach. It fell into Mr Drew's boat causing damage to a large plank. His first thought was that it would be a lot of trouble to mend it! If Reg had been in a slightly different position he would not have been here to tell the tale.

Reg recalls an enemy plane (? one brought down at Torquay on 4th September 1942) on display on the Den near the Lighthouse. It was being taken around possibly to boost morale.

Janet Roper

Janet was playing with her friends on the back beach one day when an enemy plane was heard approaching. Ern Nathan immediately shepherded the little ones to the comparative safety of his upturned boat moments before bullets began to fly.

Ken Bennett

Ken and his friends, Graham and Michael Nicholson and Gordon Grills, were fishing off the Fish Quay (known as Tank to locals) when the sound of approaching enemy aircraft made them rush for cover. As the plane flew east down river blazing machine gun fire, all the boys except Gordon ran to shelter inside some large concrete pipes stacked ready to be laid beneath the river beach. Gordon had a bite on the end of his fishing line and he did not intend to let it escape!

Ken Hexter

When I was about 7 our family lived in Saxe St. My older brothers Ron and Arthur and a lad called Owen Putt took me with them to play Pirates on an old barge moored next to Bobbett's Quay. We took two flags and attached the Union Jack to the bow and the Red Ensign to the stern. We'd been playing for some time when suddenly three German aircraft swooped overhead from the sea and began to machine-gun us.

There had been no siren - they had come in too quickly. Ron who was 11 grabbed me and whilst we ran up the beach, Putt rushed to recover the flags from either end of the barge. Arthur dived into a large concrete pipe and found a mother and very frightened young daughter already sheltering in there. An old fisherman put Ron and me in a toilet cubicle on the quay until the all-clear.

My mother decided Teignmouth was too dangerous so we spent the next two years with family at Heathfield. It was so quiet there that apart from the presence of the American Forces, nobody would have known there was a war on.

Margaret Curtis

Margaret was just a young girl when she asked her mother's permission to collect the accumulator from her uncle's garage where it was being charged up. She would walk down Third Avenue and cross over Bitton Park Rd that was fairly traffic free at that time. Her mother agreed and told Margaret to pull the front door closed on the way out and ring the bell on her return. Margaret decided otherwise and left it open. The decision may have saved her life. On the way back, an enemy plane fired a machine gun across Third Avenue. Margaret was able to run to safety through the front door. Recalling the incident in recent times, she said it was as if someone was guiding her by the hand.

Devon County Salvage Drive

An appeal from Cllr Irish appeared in the Teignmouth Post urging citizens to supply items for the Nations' salvation – Salvage. "Your bookcases must be ransacked for shell cases. Your ragbags must become blankets, uniforms and urgent field dressings. Your old rubber bottles, tyres and toys become the life-saving equipment of our airmen and sailors. Your old iron and other metals must find their way into the breeches of the guns, and your bones must be turned into explosives to fire them"

Cllr Irish's odd phrasing must be forgiven - it was doubtless penned as a matter of urgency!

Snippets

The grounds of Overcliff on Dawlish Rd and a large house called The Grotto next to the Catholic Church Hall were connected by an underground tunnel that was used as an air raid shelter by the occupants.

An armoured train was noted on one occasion when it passed through Teignmouth. The engine house was protected to hide the glow of the fire from enemy planes and the loco towed an open truck containing gun and gunner.

The US Navy had plans to convert Shaldon Bridge into a dam with sluice gates to allow for a sea plane base to be created above the bridge. Victory was won before the plan was put into action.

A large circular steel water tank for an emergency supply for fire fighting was installed at the bottom of bombed-out Gloucester Road. The tank itself was bombed during a raid.

Following several unopposed raids, the people of Teignmouth and Shaldon held a public meeting in the summer of 1942. The outcome was a petition to Winston Churchill to provide Anti-Aircraft defence. Soon afterwards, two armoured cars fitted with Bren guns were set up on Shaldon Bridge by the RAF. Sometime later, a pair of Hispanos replaced them. As the war progressed, the Bofors guns of the Royal Artillery Light Anti-Aircraft Battery helped protect the town.

Following the Blitz on Exeter in 1942, numerous shreds from copies of the Express & Echo were carried by the winds from the city and landed in Teignmouth.

John Hooper's letter about the bravery of ARP Warden Williams on page 90 records the raid on his home at 1A Barnpark Terrace. The date of the raid was 13th August 1942. John Hooper and his wife Emma survived their dreadful ordeal but would never speak of it to their daughter who experienced the raid as a toddler, or their son born in 1945. The couple lived into their 80s. Extraordinarily, John's death occurred on 13th August.

A perforated 60mm pipe was laid between Inverteign Drive and Shaldon Bridge toll house. In the event of invasion, petrol would have been pumped through the pipe and ignited to become an inpenetrable wall of fire.

A local girl looked up at a low flying enemy plane and was surprised when she saw the German pilot thumbing his nose at her!

Regiments stationed in Teignmouth

Royal Air Force
Fleet Air Arm
Royal Artillery Anti-Aircraft Batteries
Queen's Regiment -West Surrey
Buffs - Royal East Kent
Devonshire Regiment
Blackwatch - Royal Highlanders
Oxfordshire & Buckinghamshire Light Infantry
Essex Regiment
Loyal North Lancashire Regiment
Durham Light Infantry
Tower Hamlets - London Regiment

Devon County had 25 General Service Infantry Battalions of Home Guard. Newton Abbot was the 9th Battalion with seven Companies. Teignmouth, Shaldon and Bishopsteignton formed C Company under the command of Major HG Biggwither DSO Teignmouth formed 3 platoons:

No 1 Platoon *(page 38)*
Morgan Giles workforce platoon under Lt RW Broom
Electric Lighting Company's own platoon *(page 49)* under the command of Captain PS Grant

Some members of Teignmouth Home Guard moved into the 17th Royal Artillery Platoon *(Ness)* under Lt AR Drake, Lt PJ Knibbs and Captain HH Holloway.

William Lawrey

Early 1930s in Willow St and Gloucester Rd beyond. At 13, William was injured in the raid of August 1942. He was only 20 when he died in action in Malaya in 1949.

William's name was added to Teignmouth War Memorial in 1995

COUNTING THE COST ON A NATIONAL SCALE *

£11,000,000	for fighting and supply services
£2,250,000	for miscellaneous war services

Total £13,250,000   Daily War Expenditure born by the UK

At a national level, September 1940 was the worst month of the war
There were 6,954 deaths and 10,615 casualties detained in hospital
A total of 244,723 people were killed by enemy action in Great Britain
*Source: Whitaker's Almanac 1945

Remembrance Sunday 1998

The Last Word

Many, many times during the preparation of this book I shed tears of emotion, empathizing with those who lost their loved ones, homes and belongings. It is almost as if I lived through it but I was a Victory baby born 9 months after VE Day! It is impossible now to expect the young to understand the deprivations endured by those who valiantly withstood six years of hell.

Half a century of freedom and peace has turned privilege into birthright. Will this book help to open peoples' eyes to the past? I hope so, for in the past lie the answers to many questions about the future.

Thank You!

I am greatly indebted to everyone whose name appears below.
Without them Teignmouth at War might never have been published.

Founder Publication Sponsors

AEA Appleton : Valerie Ayres : John & Jeanette Bailey : Irene & Bill Bailey
Norman & Joan Bancroft : Bill & Pippa Barter : Win Barge : Margaret Bircham
Ken Boobyer : Jeffrey Boyne : Gordon Broom : John Caines : Geoff & Carmen Bartlett
Ken & Win Bennett : Mr & Mrs T Bull : Tony & Glenys Bloomfield
Anthony & Elizabeth Brenner : Jenny Brittan : Janet Burt : Jock Campbell : Cyril Carr
Rod Clark : Roy & Margaret Clarke : Cyril & Jo Coleridge : Donald & Joan Collins
Ted Collins : Mary Collins : Paul & Dawn Crawford : Paul & Yvonne Crispin : Mike Croydon
Phyllis Davey : Mr H Darling : Ron & Daphne Davies : Alf & Kathleen Dodd
Ron & Norma Doel : Peter Doel : Phyllis Drayson : Christine Franklin : Ian Frost
Neil & Colette Glasper : Tim Golder : David & Liz Golder : Hazel Godber
Patrick & Jane Gourd : Enid Goddard : Joan Guppy : John & Sue Hall
Roger & Sheila Handover : Bill Harvey : Phil & Chris Heesem : Ian & Dee Hemphill
Elizabeth Higham : Julie Hill : Diane J Hook : Sally A Hook : Amy J Hook : Dora Howells
David Hume : Denis & Neelia Hutchins : Nancy Olive Ilieve : Colin & Shirley Ingram
Edna Jenkins : Stephen Jones : Carol Jeffery : Fred & Doreen Kavanagh
Wilf, Kathy & Linda Keetch : Peter & Toni King : Tiny Knight : Anna Leatherdale
Peter & Cynthia Lewis : Molly Long : Reverends Philip & Caroline Luff : Pauline Maltby
Len & June Matthews : Ernest & Rita Menghini : Derrick & Janet Mills : Tim Mole
Robin & Peggy Mole : Joan Moyse : Susan Newbold : Frank & Hilary Nicholls
Muriel Nicholson : Meg Niblett : Fred & Margaret Niblett : Dave & Jenny Northcott
Mr & Mrs Parker : Beryl Perrett : Audrey Pope : Brian & Gwen Platt : Albert & Pat Penwill
Marjorie Phillips : Ida Percival : Dorcas Porter : Peter & Pat Prince : Margaret Quantick
Andy Ractliffe : Jillian Reed : Margaret Rees : Michael Rhys : Peter & Mary Ridler
Cllr W.Ridley : Pauline Ripley : Sheila Robbins : Don & Joan Robinson : Paula Robinson
Gordon & Brenda Roffe : Walt Rogers : Janet Roper : Sue Rose : Pauline Rossi
Bill & Sylvia Russell : Eveline Sanders : George & Sheila Scown : Bob & Peggy Seager
Pauline Seaton : Harry & Christine Sealey, : Elizabeth Sessions : Margaret Shillabeer
Sid & Barbara Skinner : John & Vanessa Silverman : James & Audrey Skerrett
Stan & Eileen Stanworth : Jim & Eileen Stowers : Arthur L Smith : Bill Studdiford
Sue Sullivan : Mary Strudwick : Joan Squire : Bill & Nell Tibbs : Ray & Peggy Thompson
Marian Tobin : Pearl Trant : Tom & Margaret Underhill : John & Angela Ward
Paul & Pat Warner : David & Marcia Weekes : Pauline Weston : Vera White
Norman White : Graham White : Geoff White : Tom & Lily Willis : John & Frances Wise
Bill & Margaret Wood : Margaret Yandell

BUSINESS

Bell Stanley : Food for Thought : John Head Finance : Grand Pier Teignmouth
Herald Express Torbay : The Endeavour Inn : Andrews Miniature World
Tibbs : Quayside Book Shop : Scott Richards : Hitchens (Devon) Ltd